The Damby Tradition of the Kono People of Sierra Leone West Africa

THE DAMBY TRADITION OF THE KONO PEOPLE OF SIERRA LEONE WEST AFRICA

With the Damby Animals as Identified by The Ancient Kono Damby Primogenitors

VOLUME II

Kumba Femusu Solleh

authorHOUSE®

AuthorHouse™
1663 Liberty Drive
Bloomington, IN 47403
www.authorhouse.com
Phone: 1-800-839-8640

First published by AuthorHouse   07/20/2011

ISBN: 978-1-4490-7466-1 (sc)
ISBN: 978-1-4490-7467-8 (ebk)

Library of Congress Control Number: 2011908785

Printed in the United States of America

CONTENTS

PART III

PART IV

PART V

PART VI

FOR OLD TIMES SAKE

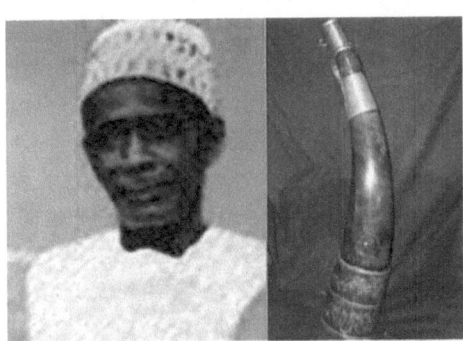

Milton Margai, first president of Sierra Leone. This original portrait of President Joseph Saidu Momoh was engraved by Czeslaw Slania, the most famous stamp engraver with over 1000 stamps to his credit. It bears his signature. For some reason the portrait was never used on any Sierra Leone bank notes or stamps. The series of bank notes issued from 1988-1993 showing Momoh's portrait were engraved by another artist, not by Slania.

There is something very unique about the portrait of President Momoh that Mr. Slania saw, but, which the Sierra Leone authority did not or did not want to see. This unique quality in the image is his "Neck", the folds of is neck depicts him as product of ancient Egyptian the *collar of his royalty which goes to show that he belong the Pharoanic bloodline of ancient Egypt. The collar or neck-line is what the African consider as a* symbol of and a sign of beauty particularly in Sierra Leone tradition. This collar emblem is also of an ancient "origin" relating to a group of personalities known as the Annanuki, entities that came to earth/Sierra Leone and resided around Bonthe area from out of space and became creator gods in the belief traditions of most global cultures as well as of most of the human religions. This image of the late president is the actual

1

representation of his physical appearance. I had the opportunity to observe him at a very closed range because he was a very close friend my uncle: LT., Tekuyamah. My uncle Tekuyamah was single male who happened to love women, therefore, as a female living in his house while attending a school, at St Joseph's Convent; I naturally became the "female" of the house.

Therefore, when Mr. Momoh, a Colonel of the Sierra Leone Army comes to visit my uncle Tekuyamah, and this was every week-end and some week-days, I was the Female in charge of his needs, and I am not talking of his Sexual needs, but making sure he gets what he needs in terms of food and drinks while my uncle supply his other needs if you know what I mean. Therefore, I had the opportunity to observe him at a very close range than most people excluding may be his wife Sissy Agnes who was also, a frequent visitor with her husband to our house. At this point, all I can say is that if the picture had been released to the general public, the Fulani Tribe of Sierra Leone would not have absorbed him through marriage to an unknown personality leading to his death in Guinea, the ancient "rout" of the "Annanukies". However, may his soul rest in perfect peace?

"This is the legacy of the African continent to the nations of the world. She has laid the cultural foundations of modern progress and therefore she and her people deserve the Honour and praise which for centuries have been falsely given to the Greeks. And like whiles, it is the purpose of this book to make this revelation the beginning of a universal reformation in race relations, which I believe would be the beginning of the solution of the problem of universal unrest."

—From *Stolen Legacy* by George G. M. James (2001:152)

DEDICATIONS

Dedicated to my parent: T. C. Solleh (Femba-Wu) and Sia Baiah Kor (Femba). The late P.C. Fasuluku I: The Great Crocodile Of Kayeema. To the late P.C. Alhajie, Sahr Tollie of Gbenseh Chiefdom

In addition, to all Kono chiefs, past and present. Last but not the least, to Tumoeh, The Genie of my lamp.

What is the Pope's motive (motif)?

The Pope headdress and the British West African Penny.

SEE THE COSMOLOGY OF THE KONO PEOPLE OF SIERRA, WEST AFRICA BY KUMBA F. SOLLEH FOR ANSWERS.

FOREWORD

In the writing of this book, in order to present a true picture of my culture as well as the origins and history of my people, I have included data that might be of an esoteric and occult nature. Also, I have presented theories that could be controversial and might even offend some people. This was not my intention, as my objective is to present facts, and if this presentation of facts has resulted in any kind of offense, I offer my sincerest apologies.

In the writing or documentation of any history or culture, truth has to be preserved, and if truth is not preserved correctly, then the writing will not be accurate. Truth means many things to many people, but it is still truth. And as truth has inestimable value, it should never be regarded as personal offense. Time has a natural warp, and to discover reality across the centuries is very difficult. So much has been lost. So much has been altered, and so much has been suppressed.

In particular, when you are writing anything of any value about the historical nature of Africa, one always runs into many difficulties because of (1) the tremendous amounts of distortion as a result, (2) the loss of documentation, knowledge, and true cultural account, all of which now lay buried in the vast desert of the Sahara, and (3) the severe fragmentation of African history. It is no coincidence that Africa is called the "Dark Continent," and because truth must be told, Africa is going to remain a dark continent unless her children are allowed to freely report the historical nature of their people without bias. Written documents are frequently written from the standpoint of the writer, and writers have proved to be one-sided. This author writes from a multi-faceted standpoint. She uses a diamond pen. Truth is truly a diamond.

For any reader or interested party to say the truth of African history is correct from his or her perspective is a fallacy, because he

7

or she is doing exactly what the author could be accused of doing. Furthermore, not to report a narrative as you know it to be true is "living a lie," or as an African would say, "hiding behind your finger" or "eating the monkey and rejecting the tail."

The pursuit of truth should be truth, and there has been no other objective in the writing of this book.

Much is not known about the Kono tribe, even though the Kono district of Sierra Leone is producing one-third of the world's supply of diamonds. It's this author's intention to introduce the Kono people as a historical entity, as important members of the world community, as a people with a past and a future in the global network. Thus, I now introduce you to the Kono people of Sierra Leone, West Africa.

At the end of every age, there must come a time for the clarification of all that had been misunderstood or misinterpreted before. Otherwise, we as humans in our unfoldment would never be able to extricate ourselves from the net of illusion and faulty teachings that have held us in bondage. And we see signs indeed that we have questioned things at the end of the age. They are all around and about us.

Some of these signs are showing us that we are now in the "latter days," that the vast amount of new age teachings that are certainly being expounded through the lips and writings of philosophers and other thinkers are questionable. And the young are refusing to accept the antiquated religious and cultural concepts of their elders, and they are beginning to study occultism and the hidden mysteries of life.

For instance, the two Kono secret societies, the Poro and the Sandeh, have many members, but only a few know the real secret teachings behind the society. Even the old men of our times are now only starting to embark into the realms of the unknown in the constant search to discover the laws that govern time and space, thus gaining control over the lives of the people they govern and guide. Yes, indeed, the walls of materialism and the traditions of our elders are tumbling down fast, but the teachings and philosophies of the Kono have withstood the test of time. The wisdom of our elders is on the increase, and cultural beliefs are as old as life itself.

This is so because many seekers of truth are now expressing the "soul awakening."

There is an inscription on the walls of Delphi and it reads, *"Man, known thyself and then thou will know the universe and the gods."*

This book, which covers the lives of tenacious initiations, also tends to indicate that we are now in the clarification period. Thus, it is good to remember that the temples are open to release the higher esoteric teachings to the public, which has not always been the case in history.

PREFACE

After I have given you information about the Kono naming and Damby traditions, I shall, in fact, attempt to disclose and go beyond the local and temporal differences in cults and dogmas and look for those trends and qualities that seem to have shaped the character of the ancient Kono beliefs as a whole.

The Kono beliefs were rooted in a single basic conviction: their universe, which they call "*Dunya*," is essentially changeless. Therefore, it is irrelevant that their views seem untenable to us. What is relevant here is that the Kono held it and that it formed not only their religious belief but also their moral and political philosophy.

I undertook this task (writing and researching the origin of the Kono words) on the premise that it justified my method, which is studying etymology. By this I mean, the study of the meaning of the Kono words, or part of the words and how the words have arrived at their current form and meaning. Etymology often shows the different forms the word has taken in passing from one language to another, and sometimes shows related words in other languages, and this is why some words have the same spelling but different history of origin. For example, Greek culture borrowed many African words, which they incorporated into their common language, which they call Koine or the common Greek language. (See my first book, *Kono Gold or Koine Gold*)

Through my method of research, I demonstrate that ancient thought can be comprehended once its own peculiar coherence is understood. Through the same method, Kono culture can be discovered through the understanding, interpretation, and application of the various Kono words in relationship to the Damby animals, the basic understanding of the ten naming traditions, and the basic counting systems. Therefore, I have reduced critical remarks to a minimum.

As was previously discussed, the Kono philosophy seems to view the universe or Dunya as equilibrium of opposites. Thus, they were preoccupied with death.

As my father pointed out, the Kono considered death an interruption but not an end of life, which continues at *Yardu* (god's town). Death for the Kono is a change in the individual personality, not its annihilation. This belief in existence of life after death is shown by what the West called ancestor worship. A Kono would call his or her dead relative to arbitrate between the individual and others or to ask his or her dead relative to help rescue their needs from adverse effects of everyday living.

THE CONCEPT OF DAMBY ANIMALS AS POWER ANIMALS.

The wisdom and knowledge of ancient Damby Traditions are being revived in the West as healing techniques under varieties of names, such as shamanic traditions. Here, an introduction to shamanism and Damby tradition is briefly stated to let the reader know that all ancient belief systems is **One** for it came down to us from a common source, the Annunaki as stated below; and the understanding of this truth can restore us to wholeness.

WHAT IS SHAMANISM?

Shamanism like Damby Tradition dates back to some thousands of years and is the first spiritual practice known to the world because it linked us to our ancient Creator Masters, now known as the Annunaki. The word Shamanism comes from the word *"semen"* referring to the male energy of creation; this is what is commonly referred to as the sperm.

This word, 'Shamanism' also relate to the word 'She-Man' (Xi-Man), hence the concept and reality of mystical *androgyny* was central to the practice of the shaman and esoteric magicians. The word 'She-Man' (Xi-Man) is still used among the Temne tribe of Sierra Leone as a name for a new graduate from the female secret society call 'bondo'

Shamanism can be used by anyone as a problem-solving technique if it is understood and translated into modern times; genetic engineering. and DNA research programs present sufficient evidence for this claim.

The word "shaman" is said to have originated from the Tungusic language of Siberia.

However, this may be false, because as the African Tradition shows; the word has a feminine concept which links the word to the ancient people of West Africa. Shamanism is still been practiced around the globe.

This practice ranges from the Chomah (Kono word for healers also known as witch doctors) to the medicine men of native North and South America. In addition, among the healers are the Noaidi of the Sámi tradition of the Northern belt of Europe stretching from Norway to Siberia including the aborigines in Australia? The practice is also seen among the priests of Korea and Hawaii. Shamans are known to be the first healers of humankind.

Most animistic traditions are shamanic in nature and are globally distributed; they use power animals for energy, guidance and help. When a child is born, one or more power animals take care of them in the spiritual world. For example, the bear helps children to come into this world. There are many stories in all global cultures telling us of animals adopting and nursing children as if the child was one of their own. For example, Ramous and Romulus; and Tarzan to name only but a few of stories we read in which human children were adopted by animals as one of their own. Why do you think that teddy bears are so popular amongst children around the world? In the Kono Damby Tradition Children are born into their Damby animals, thus, a child's dream of animals is always taken to mean a thing of importance.

Children still have a natural feeling and intuition to correspond with the other world. It is we, the adults, who lose touch with this natural phenomenon and dismiss our children's attempts to tell us about their conversations with animals in their dreams.In the shamanic tradition, a shamanic practitioners can help an individual to find his spiritual power animal or connect him or her with his or her guardian so the individual can access them throughout his or her life.

Some of us may need the energy of a tiger to regain control in today's difficult world; others would benefit from the power of the alpha wolf (the dog or *Yimineh* Damby) to become a leader and protector; it could also happen that an elephant (Kama Damby) will show up to bring light and total well being into the life of those it chooses.The shaman can help those who need to make a clear decision, but are confused by the options available by sending the power of the *Siimbii* the Kono word for eagle (Kondaih Damby).

Power or Damby Animals were not chosen without any reason; animals are mostly representatives of wild animal species because domesticated animals do not have enough power as they have given up control over their life.

Birds or fish can also be power animals, but insects or spiders with the exception of honeybees that is depicted as signifying immortality and resurrection, were royal emblems of the Merovingian, revived by Napoleon. The bee is heraldic emblem too of the Barberini. Otherwise insects do not really qualify as helpers from the other world. Mostly people have one or two power animals at a time, but people can also have access to plenty of them through their Damby connection.

The Damby Traditions as strict dietary laws. The Damby animals are emblematic of our male ancestral Damby founders who do not live because we are etched in their DNA or is it us that are etched in their DNA?

Unlike the Damby Tradition, there are no rules in the shamanic world. Everyone makes his or her own experiences and these are neither right nor wrong. Sometimes, a power animal leaves the individual and is replaced by another protector that protects the well being of the individual in times of need. The shaman unlike the Damby Tradition the individual in time of a crisis he may lose his soul power or give it away voluntarily.

SPIRITUAL GUARDIANS

Both the Damby Tradition and the Shamanic Tradition believe that helpers in the other world appear either as power animals, plant human or god-like forms. Your guardian angel can also present itself in some other form totally different from the forms listed above.

ACKNOWLEDGMENTS

Acknowledgments must be given first and foremost to God Almighty and to the dearly departed souls who left their valuable knowledge, which is now unfolding in this book.

Special thanks to Mary Munro, an award-winning poet, without whose help this book would never have been written. Thanks for her tireless typing, research, grammatical editing, and more.

But one general acknowledgment must be made here to Erik Molano, due to his help with the cover design and some proofreading.

I would also like give thanks to my dear friend Dr. Ernie Smith, a comparative linguistics consultant, without whose linguistic knowledge the skeletal structure of this book would never have taken shape. I owe him my gratitude, and I will never be able to pay him back. Thus, I recommend his book on the Egyptian etymology of the 'N' word, *Nigger—A Divine Origin*, published by Milligan Books in 2003.

Thanks go to my two children, Ali Kai Bindi and Baiah-Kor Feyah Esther Morsay, whose love and help gave me the courage to press on in spite of the obstacles. Also, I thank my four grandchildren, Sia Janaiah Morsay, Marcus Sahr Bindi, Irain Tamba Bindi, and Chi-Chi whose love knows no bounds. I also thank the rest of my family members for continued emotional support.

I give special acknowledgment to all the children who lost their lives during the Blood Diamond Conflict in Sierra Leone, West Africa. For these people, especially the children, who were forbidden by some unforeseen energy to see their own "unbecoming." Remember children, life is an everlasting circle with no beginning and, therefore, no end. Death is neither the end all nor the beginning of all. Death says, "I am the beginning and the end. No one goes to the source but through the Almighty. I am today, tomorrow, and yesterday. I am the Lord of eternity of all initiations. Yes, I am." The process of conquering death has created more problems than solutions, for the problem with killing death results in creating more death. The only solution is to wait for death to wear itself out. Is this not what the Kono word *Konu* means?

As a Damby member, I write this book for you, as a touch to enable you to find your way home. ***May their souls rest in perfect peace.***

PROLOGUE

Ancient Egypt's Contribution to West African Religions

KAMITIC (GREEK EGYPTIAN) CONTRIBUTION TO THE HUMAN CIVILIZATION

Human history has shown time and time again that the Egyptians our <u>mentors</u>, had devised a myth, enacted in the heavens yet paralleled in common with human experience as evidenced in the Kono Damby Tradition shown in the pages of this book. However, as in all ancient Mystery Cultures, to understand and use the teachings, one has to become an initiate in one of the many schools available in one's community or go in search of one that best fits one's needs. This is exactly what I did; I came to the USA with a purpose in mind: "to rediscover myself in order to rediscover the Kono people.

This search of the self before searching the self of other is one of the major reasons why all prophets from the ancient Hebrew Damby had to go to Ancient Egypt, the Land they referred to as the land of *"Bondage"* even if, it **meant "pimping" their wives as was the case with** *"the "supposed" father of all Nations"*, Abraham, his *grand son Isaac and other family members*.

However, the Hebrews never really mastered the mysteries until Moses and therefore, He (Moses) was given the Exodus movement of the Israelite Damby to the promise land with ease.

WHY DID THE OTHERS BEFORE MOSES FAILED BUT HE WAS GIVEN THE EXODUS?

Moses succeeded because he studied the history of his people.

Moses knew that the best time to achieve financial wealth is during the time of hunger, hardship or famine. Therefore, Moses had to study six historical personalities before him. To make a point I will briefly examine these six persons through the words of the Holy Bible.

Thus, I present Abraham and the history of . . .

THE SIX ANCIENT HISTORICAL PEOPLE WHO GOT WEALTHY DURING FAMINE

1) ABRAHAM

"The lord said to Abraham: "Get out of your country. From your family (Gen. 13:5), And from your father's house, to a land that I will show you. I will make you a great nation; I will bless you (Deut. 26:5). And your name great; and you shall be a blessing. I will bless those who bless you. And I will curse him who curses you; (Num.24:9. And in you all the families of the earth shall be blessed". See Genesis 12: 1-3, So Pharaoh commanded his men concerning him; and they sent him away, with his and all that he had. Here, we see Abraham leaving Egypt with all the wealth of the Egyptian Pharaoh, Why?

ISAAC/JACOB

"There was a famine in the land besides the famine that was in days of Abraham. And Isaac went to Abimelech King of the Philistines, in Gerar. (Gen.12:10). Then the Lord appeared to him and said: Do not go down to Egypt; live in the land of which I will tell (Genesis 12:7, 18:1, 35:9 and Gen. 12:1. Dwell in this land, and I will be with you and bless you; for unto you and your descendants I give all these lands, and I will perform the oaths which I swore to

Abram your father." . . . So Isaac dwelt in Gerar . . . Gen.35. (See Genesis 26)

GENESIS 12

2) ISAAC

GENESIS 26

3) JACOB

Genesis 31: 1 *through* 55
"Now Jacob heard the words of Laban's sons, saying, "Jacob has taken away all was our father's and from what was our father's he has acquired all this wealth" . . . Then the Lord said to Jacob, Return to the land of your fathers and to your family, and I will be with you . . . (*Genesis 28:15, 20, 21; 32:9; Genesis 46:4*) . . . "Genesis 31: 9 So God has taken away the live-stock of your father and given them to me" . . ." (Gen. 28:1 & 29:11.)

4) JOSEPH

Genesis 41:1 *through* 57
". . . verse 41 "And the Pharaoh said to Joseph, "see I have set you over all the land of Egypt". Then the Pharaoh took of his signet ring off his hand and put it on Joseph's hand; and he clothed him in garments of fine linen and put a gold chain around his neck". "And he had him ride in the second chariot which he had; and they cried out before him, "*Bow the knee!*" So he set him over all the land of Egypt". (Gen. 42:6; 46:29. Esther 6:9).

5) ISRAEL

Exodus12:1 *through* 51
". . . 21 Then Moses called all the elders of Israel and . . ." pick out and take lambs for yourselves according to your families . . ." *verse 35* . . . the children of Israel have done according to words of Moses . . . the Egyptians silver, gold, and clothing." *Verse 36* . . .

God had given . . . thus they plundered the Egyptians." [(*Ex. 3:21; 15:14*) . . ."]

6) SOLOMON

1king 10:23 "So, "King Solomon surpassed all the kings of the earth in riches and wisdom." (1 king 3:12; 13; 14:30).

WHO WILL BE THE *7TH* PERSONALITY NEXT?

The ancient Egyptian used certain symbols to communicate to other initiates regarding the ideas and meanings behind the three Aspects of consciousness used by humans on Earth. These symbols are covered in other volumes of the Damby series. However, brief introduction of the concepts are discussed below.

Nonetheless, of all ancient civilizations on planet Earth, the ancient Kamitic (Egyptian) civilization lasted longer than any other in recorded history did. The Kamitic civil calendar, being the oldest in recorded history, originated about four millennia before Christ. The exact date of its origin is unknown.

However, it is believed by most historians that Imhotep, anciently known as the supreme official of King Djoser in c.2670 BC, was a great influence behind the implementation of the calendar.

The Egyptian calendar is a solar calendar that consists of 12 months in a year with 30 days (3 decans of 10 days each) and 5 additional yearly days (*epagomenes*, the five extra days were considered to be "out side of time', as the Birthdays of the five *Neteru*/gods, *Asar, Ast, Heru, Nebhet* and *Set*) for a total of 365 days.

The myth surrounding the creation of the calendar goes something like this . . . **Nut,** goddess of the Sky, was separated from her lover **Geb**, (*the Kono word for this goddess is still Tegbeh, Gebeh or Chebeh, the combined shortened form is Bete-eh* chosen or assigned to females as an initiation name, usually given to female named Sia to be forever called Sia bete-eh) god of the Earth, and cursed with barrenness:

According to the ancient narratives **Nut,** goddess of the Sky could not give birth in any month of the year. Therefore, *Djehuti,* (note here that the Kono word for penis is che-eh, or djeh, the Kono word for 'head', the head of the penis is *djeh-khu-neh'*, Thus, the word *djekhu-nti or Djehuti, means 'the owner of the head of the penis"*, who was also known as the *moon-god of time, measurement and wisdom*. He also proceeds over females' menstrual cycles, thus as the myth states he decided to help Nut and Geb.

To achieve this task, *Djehuti* challenged the reigning gods, thus, in a game of dice, he won five extra days not belonging to any particular month, and these five days were then given to the couples, which Nut used to produce five children, including *Ast (Isis) and Asar (Osiris)*.

In the Kono Damby Tradition, this was the origin of the Kono word *Sandu-u, meaning five moons or five year circle* (**San**-in Kono was the ancient name for the moon). The word **Sandu-U** should have been the name assigned to the Dog Damby, but instead it was assigned to Leopard Damby. The Kono name for Dog *is Oyo-o, woo or wu-u*. I know this as a fact because my father is of the Leopard and therefore all his children belong to the Leopard Damby call *Sandu-u-nu,* one of the three groups of the leopard Damby. One of my Sisters is called Finda **Sandu-u-gbaa-ah**; she is now known by most people as Leticia.

HELICAL RISING

According to Plutarch, "Sirius" was consecrated to Ast/Isis, for it brings the water (Menstrual blood). Compare the name Sirius to the name Sandu-u.

The **Kamu (ancient Egyptians)** had a 'sacred' calendar that was utilized by the Priest and *Per Aa* (Pharaoh) which is *Fah-rah, or Phah-waah*. This was an astronomical calendar, based on **the heliacal rising of Sirius**, the brightest star in the sky, at the dawn of the eastern horizon, this was the star called *Sandu-uh* and for the Kono, it is associated with the Dog and the Leopard . . . My father is from the Leopard Damby and my mother is from the Dog Damby called Yimine-nu, this, the Dogons of Mali refer to as Yimiyah. There is a revelation regarding my father's nick-name for me, which is 'Koh'. *The Leopard and the dog both belong to the Dog Star anciently known as* **Koh.** Been born borne in dual set, male and female set,

21

put me in a place of cosmic protection as understood by the, those the name "Sothis', another ancient name for that same star can easily by interpreted as the Kono name *Sokoh for the parallel each other.*

A helical rising of a star is defined as its appearance above the horizon just before sunrise. The day on which the heliacal rising of Sirius occurs marks the first day of the year and the beginning of the actual Inundation (as opposed to the calendrical one).

The word Inundation is defined as an accumulation of an overwhelming amount of things that somebody has to deal with such as flood.

Sirius, Sothis or Spdt in Ancient Egypt is characterized by high luminosity and is a member of the constellation called *Canis Major,* (the great Dog). *Yiminneh* or *Yeemineh* is the Kono name for this Star or Planet.

To commemorate this name, the Kono Tradition assigned the name *Yeemineh* to the clan of Dogs, thus, a Kono Damby animal is called Yemineh. This is what the Dogons of Mali, West Africa call Yemiyah). It lies about 8.6 light years from earth.

The first day coincides with the arrival of the highest point of the Nile flood at Memphis, south west of Cairo, the capital of Egypt during the early dynastic period of the Old Kingdom.

The helical rising of Sirius coincides with the new year's day of the civil calendar which occurs every 1461 years which are equal to 365¼ days (the length of years which became **the Julian year**). This is a period of 533,265 days, which has been historically dubbed a 'Sothic Cycle,' because *Sothis* is the Greek name of Sirius.

The term Sokoh, a Kono name for the first female twin born in a set of more than one female in a set also means a star. The name *Sokoh* is also represented among rocks under the name of *Kohkabah.* Later the name Kohkabah became Kabanah, Khabanakoh or Kanab, all relating to Serpent and therefore, Lunar, as well as Feminine name.

The Egyptian civilization lived through several such cycles. There was a 3rd century A.D record: known as <u>grammarian Censorinus</u> which stated that, in A.D. 139, the first day of the Egyptian Civil Year coincided with the helical rising of Sirius, marking the end of a Sothic cycle.

Ancient Rome celebrated this phenomenon of <u>the heliacal rising</u> by issuing minted coins on the reversed side of which appears the Greek inscription *A ION,* An ancient Roman word indicating *"an end of an Era".* The Kono meaning for the word *"A ION"* is, 'it has gone in . . .' or 'it has set', this meanings depicts the 'sun-set', a symbol of Death and resurrection'.

Egypt then was under the Roman Rule of Emperor Antoninus Pius. The notion of eternal time was personified and deified. A relief of the deity **Aion** was found in Oxyrhnichus, present day el-Bahnasa in middle Egypt.

The word **A-ion** is actually a Kono word also meaning *"to spoil it"* or *"to Destroy it",* it is a command word. **A-yohn** *or A-ion is the Kono word for "to break it, spoiled it, to put an end to it or damage it.* Hence our present civilization has arrived at apoint in time where mighty men of power and greed command this sacred word *"A ION"* to achieve what ever they desire through the use of agents.

These agent can destroy anything and any where in the world via certain devices such as 'virtual reality or virtual presentation',

These agents, who act as the "Kickers" of the agenda, go by another name which we ignorantly refer to as "secret agents". These secret agents or *"armature actors* are briefly examined below.

The phrase **AR·MA·TURE** keeper for magnet, refers to a bar of soft iron or steel placed across the poles of a magnet to maintain its strength, these are the characteristics of the mind control *secret agents* assigned over our lives. The phrase also applies in ELECTRICAL ENGINEERING AND MEANS the moving part in an electromagnetic device, wound with coils that carry a current.

Within the armature controller agents are sometimes sub-agents with special kinds of functions who are completely un-aware of other groups from the same agency. To understand the mechanics of these agents is to envision them as a device in a generator, an electric current is induced in the coils (of a serpent) when they revolve through a magnetic field.

THESE AGENTS CAN ALSO BE VIEWED IN THE FUNCTIONS FOR THE 'ELITES' FROM A BIOLOGICAL ASPECT, AS protective outer covering or structure e.g. quills on a porcupine or spines on a plant or the spinal cord. They can also be examined from the art of SCULPTURED framework for model: a framework that supports a sculpture while it is being modeled (someone who is easy to manipulate).

To most of theses groups, they have been trained to see anyone outside their group as an enemy. Nonetheless, this **A ION** concept found its way into Persian, Mithraism, later into Gnosticism and finally kicked into our present usage under the guises of the word armature (army-armed-structure).

Before proceeding further with the discussion on the AION concept, I must call your attention to an observation below . . . to three words: *Baffin, Bayah or Bayawah and Bagbeh.*

In the Kono District of Sierra Leone there are three Tributaries of Rivers called *Baffin, Bayah or Bayawah and Bagbeh that parallel the tributaries of ancient Egypt's Nile river . . .*

These three Rivers: *Baffin* (Black Ba or Mother), **Bayawah** (Mighty Eye, or the 'Red' Mother; here, **Bayah** means the Eyes of the Mother), and **Bagbeh** (the White Mother).

This author's ancient village is still situated on the corners of River *Baffin and River Bayah or Bayawah* respectively.

Therefore I posit a question, *why would the Ancient Kono name their Rivers in color; Black, Red and White? Could this be their way of remembering the lands they were forced to leave? Remember here that there is no distinction made in shades of colors between blue, black and other dark colors, to the Kono they will all be called "black", thus, the Blue Nile would be called Black Nile.*

Before the construction of the Aswan High Dam in 1961, the inundations of the Nile were a yearly phenomenon, caused by the summer rains over the Ethiopian highlands, which are drained *by two of the three major tributaries of the Nile:* the *Blue Nile* and *the Black Nile.*

The **Blue** Nile (*Gihon*) flows from Lake *Tana* (a Kono word meaning prohibition) and joins **the White Nile** at Khartoum to form the Nile proper, whereas the **Black Nile** (Atbarah or Atbara) is the only tributary of the Nile after Khartoum. As you see, Kamet like the Kono District had Rivers named in colors: the <u>Black Nile</u>, the <u>White Nile</u> and the <u>Blue Nile</u>

Coincidence or facts of History?

The *Black Nile* like the *Baffin* river in the Kono District is dry for most of the year, but in a few short months during the raining

24

seasons it provides over 20% like river Baffin, of the Nile's total yearly volume of water, loaded with about 11 million tons of this black mud which once made Egypt fertile, but is now settling in Lake Nasser, behind the Aswan Dam.

The *White Nile* carries only half the total flow of the *Blue Nile* but it's much more regular. It flows from Lake Tanganyika (Victoria), under a succession of names. The *Kagera* River flows into Lake Tanganyika/Victoria, and has an upper branch, the *Ruvyironza* River of Burundi, whose source is now considered to be the ultimate source of the Nile.

I must mention here that the rivers Baffin and Bayah or Bayawah merge at my village and together they flow to join River Bagbeh at N'jaiama Sewah-fe area.

Is it not rather odd that the ancient River call Nile has the same number, color descriptions, and functions parallel those of the three Rivers in the Kono District of Sierra Leone as explained above?

Nonetheless, the exact day when a heliacal rising is observed may depend on the longitude and latitude of the observer. The altitude is somewhat relevant too (on the equator, a star rising due east would be seen from a 100m cliff about 76.8s earlier than from the beach). The brightness of the star is important as well, since fainter objects disappear earlier at dawn. An intercalary day is a day added to the calendar year to keep calendar years concurrent with solar years. In the Gregorian calendar February 29 is an intercalary day in leap years.

THE MOTTO OF THE SERPENT

"That which is above is like that which is below, and that which is below is like that which is above for the accomplishment of the wonders of one thing."

"Its father is the Sun; its mother is the Moon; the earth is her nurse, she gets her breath from the belly of the wind.

"It is the Universal Principle; the Talisman of the World."

(The ancient serpent, is the creative principle, the God of all initiates)

"The Serpent, inspirer of disobedience, of insubordination, and of revolt, was cursed by ancient Theocrats, although it was honored among initiates."

"To become like unto Divinity, such was the goal of the Ancient mysteries. To-day the program of initiation has not changed, the serpent does not believe in dog-mas.

READER ALERT:

Some Legal Issues Involved in the Damby Tradition

In this Second Volume, I will discuss some of the legal *issues involving the Kono Damby Tradition.* To do this successfully, I will revisit the Book of Ruth and other books of the Holy Bible. The reason for this is due to the fact that we Africans have been lead to believe that the bible is foreign to Africans even though 90% of the Old Testament Traditions parallel the Kono Damby Tradition as shown in this book. One of such ancient Biblical Traditions that parallels the Kono Damby tradition is the Levirate Law, which is claimed to be Jewish but which in fact, is Kono.

PART I

GENERAL INTRODUCTION

*Mother's Milk: The Bases For Swoon-Yu-U
in the Kono Damby Tradition*

HUMAN SKELETON AND APE SKELETONS

The human body is a hologram in which the creator projects or expresses her/ his ideas and designs her effort to communicate to the external spheres of her creation, *"Let us make man in our image after our likeness"* was the first clue given to humanity of the creators' intent to share of herself.

Compare these two skeletons and see the truth of being created in the creator's image and likeness. With careful assessment and observation you realize the phrase *". . . man in our image and likeness"*, This will bring your animal sides come into play.

It is on the bases of this realization of our true nature: that every human has an animal characteristics or side that the Kono formulated their Damby Tradition.

MALE AND FEMALE GENDER DIFFERENTIATIONS

PENIS (pen-is), the real or proper name for this physiological structure is *Pen-Is*; and its meaning is this: *Physiology expresses and notes in sign language or symbols*. In other words, the penis is a pen through which the creators express themselves at least according to the male primogenitors. Like a pen, it must have a liquid or ink that acts as a <u>catalyst</u> to bring the Creators' ideas to manifestations. It is this liquid called sperm, the water that waters the Garden of Eden'. In other words a sperm is <u>a substance that increases the rate</u>

of a chemical reaction without itself undergoing any change in the Historical Womb of the creator.

VAGINA: like the penis analogy, the word vagina means, *Vision Aligns Graphical Ideas and Notes to the Alphabets*. The Alphabets are the seeds, the Hieroglyphic planted in the Historical Womb of Mother Nature, the Garden of Eden that gave birth to the Pyramids, the Universal laboratory from *when's* all that is created were first incubated.

The vagina expresses matter and unites ideas of the alphabet or hieroglyphics into form such as children that the creator wishes to express.

DAMBY: *The Divine Alignments of Matter brings Unity of the Ones within the creation.* All cultures of the world have some animals or other creatures as symbolism of divinity. The reason is that the forms and habits of these creatures and the media in which they exist closely relate them to the various generative and germinative powers of Nature and were viewed as evidence of the omnipresence.

The ancient Philosophers and Scientists understood that all life form has its origin in water. Thus, some ancient cultures chose the fish as the symbol of the life germ. The fish chosen by the Kono is *Sa-nneh (eel)*; this interprets to mean that *'Sa, the ancient God is here'*

THE BASES FOR SWOON-YU-U IN THE KONO DAMBY TRADITION

To understand the Kono Damby Tradition one must first understand other Kono word, which the Kono call **swoon-y-u-u**, the bases of the Kono Damby Tradition. The *swoon-y-u-u* concept is determined by two factors as follows:

1) "SUNN-SUNHN". THE "BREAST MILK", (BOBBY-WATER) OF THE MOTHER DETERMINES EXISTENCE.

2) THE TOTEMIC PROHIBITION OF THE FATHER

WHAT BREAKS THE SWOON-YU-U TIES?

One, LEGAL IMPLICATIONS
Two, INCESTIOU BEHAVIOURS
Three, VIOLATIONS OF DAMBY EXPECTATIONS

What is the Damby Dietary Law?

DAMBY OR CLAN NAMING SYSTEM OR THE NAMING SYSTEM BASED ON DIETARY LAWS.

In my first book *Kono Gold or Koine Gold* by *Kumba K. Solleh*, I established that among the Kono, the Naming System of persons is based about the pregnancies of the mother because it is only women, who get pregnant. Here I am going to talk on another Naming System that combines with the birth names to give an individual his or her full identity in time and space. *This is what the Kono call the Damby.*

In my second book THE DAMBY SYSTEM OF THE KONO PEOPLE (CONCEPTS OF FAMILY WITH SPECIAL EMPHASIS ON STRICT DIETARY LAWS)' I explained that the words *Damby* and *clan* though closely interrelated are not identical. While both Damby and clan developed from a family unit, each has its distinct scope. In the *Damby Tradition,* a family is bilateral since it has a male member, the father and a female member the mother. *A clan*, however, is a family group, propagated and expanded from a single lineage, male or father—line. In other words, a clan is a group formed by descendants of a single lineage. Moreover, it can therefore be called, a patrilineal community.

A Damby differs from clan-ship in that it is patrilineal and not confined to a single lineage.

In this third book, Volume three of the Damby Tradition I am establish *that since* the Damby Tradition is based primarily on genetic and bloodline of the biological parents, a genetic and bloodline solution is needed to settle the issue of the Primogeniture.

In a broader sense Damby is not only composed of paternal and maternal lines it also has children from previous marriages of the wives especially if biological fathers did not establish their legal rights. *The thing that holds and ties the Damby into a single bond is the dietary laws that are rooted in genetics and bloodline of both parents particularly the father's bloodline.* The concept of clan and Damby are fully illustrated in all my books.

The Damby therefore, is a group of people within a tribe who are bonded based on totemic, magical religious belief and practice of which the uniting force is the association with dietary usually animals and vegetable laws. Here the paternal family line is the Damby. The paternal line is not always based on kinship but on the laws of Damby of the person's totemic diet, that is his or her biological father's. Nevertheless, when a man marries a woman with children the children are automatically of the Damby.

Damby Mansa is the head of the Damby and is the oldest living male member of the Damby. The Damby Mansah also acts as the priest in cases of violation of the food taboo.

The Kono word for taboo is **tana**. People let others know of their **tana** during a sneeze. The reason is this, when a person sneezes, it is a common practice to name ones **tana** or forbidden food usually animal. For example, when I sneeze I am supposed to say, *"I do not eat leopards" at the end of every sneeze.* This let others know my Damby, which may save me in case of need. This is especially helpful if one is a stranger in a strange environment. Others, who may hear your tana may be of your **Damby;** and therefore may give you all the assistance you may need. A **tana** given under any other circumstance will perhaps not get such a favorable reception. Damby were originally territorial but are now scattered. The Damby is illustrated below as follow

DAMBY OR THE DIETARY LAW NAMES

Therefore, in a way people are born into their names and Damby. It is not by a strange coincident that we are thought in our educational institutions that every human being has a genetic maker visa—vies the DNA of protein chains from where every human or every living creature get its hereditary traits. By also a similar education, we are told, *"you are what you eat".*

In a simple definition then, I am saying that our heredity marker, the DNA is nothing but foods we eat which over time became concentrated in the vessel of the blood as DNA. Heredity or family trait is in terms of dietary aspects is determined by the diets of the family. Because certain families became a custom to particular foods in such a way that without that particular food even for a day will have a discomforting effects on the individual family.

In this section of the book, I am attempting to address legal issues that cause the Damby break-up.

CHAPTER ONE

Swoon-Yu-U

SWOON-YU-U FORMS A DAMBY GROUP

WHO ARE THE PRIMOGENITORS?

The defining features of the Primogenitors are given and explained above. However, the source of their concept of a Damby group must be presented in order to understand the bases for their choice of Laws that govern the Damby Tradition.

To understand the Kono Damby Tradition one must first understand an other Kono word, which the Kono call **swoon-y-u-u**, the bases of the Kono Damby Tradition. The *swoon-y-u-u* concept is determined by two main factors as follows:

1) "SU-U-SUH" YEE OR SWOO-SWOOH-YEEH (THE "BREAST MILK", (BOBBY-WATER) OF THE MOTHER THAT DETERMINES EXISTENCE.

2) THE TOTEMIC PROHIBITION OF THE FATHER

Furthermore, to understand the meaning of the word, *"Sun-yu-u"*, the word must be broken into its component parts as follows: *Sunn or Swoon* is a Kono word that means, "To be born". *Suun-yu-u or swoon-yu-u* depicts a biological cord, rope, thread or string that binds individuals together in a group or family.

LAMINA-PROTEIN

By this, I mean that the word *Sun-yu—or swoon-yu-u* is that third force that is at the root of family unit or relationship. For example, the test of the concept of **Swoon-yu-u** is presented when there is a death in a family, usually the time for family to get together and support each other.

This process of getting together results in the concert of heart forming that acts as a directional force, a "key" to establish proper family relationship ties that binds the individuals or groups to each other in love. This is what the Kono call **Swoon-yu-u** *or* **sun-yu-u**, this word means a 'thing' or substance that binds or holds 'family 'thread', 'rope', 'string' or 'cord' together. It is this binding ability of the protein, the accumulated energy source from foods we eat.

This means that our diets especially protein-diet produces a substance that parallels the Kono Damby concept of **Swoon-yu-u**, the "thing" that holds us together structurally.

"SU-U-SUH". THE "BREAST MILK", (BOBBY-WATER) OF THE MOTHER DETERMINES EXISTENCE

The Kono word for breast is *"Su-su-uh"* or *'swoo-swooh'* and the word for Breast-Milk is ***"Su-su-uh-Yeeh"*** or ***swoo-swooh-yeeh,*** meaning breast water. The Kono word for 'to be borne' is *'Su-unh'*, whilst the word for ancient is also ***"Suu-hnn" or "Sunn-sunhn"***.

The word ***"Sunn-sunhn"*** depicts the forcefulness of expression to indicate the importance of something. On the other hand, The word ***sunn-suhn*** emphasis the time—line in question.

In modern research in genetics, a finding has been established as follows:

MATRILINEALITY

Marilineality is a system in which one belongs to one's mother's lineage.

A matriline is a line of descent from a female ancestor to a descendant (of either sex) in which the individuals in all intervening generations are female. In a matrilineal descent system (uterine descent), an individual is considered to belong to the same descent group as his or her mother. This is in contrast to the more common pattern of patrilineal descent.

The uterine ancestry of an individual is a person's pure female ancestry, i.e., a matriline leading from a female ancestor to that individual.

Mitochondrial DNA (mt-DNA) is normally inherited exclusively from one's mother—both daughters and sons inherit it all the same. As mt-DNA is sort of "cellular power plants," one's metabolism and energy conversion are much influenced by the matrilineal descent.

In some cultures, membership of a group is inherited matrilineally, examples of this include many ancient cultures such as the Egyptians and contemporary ones such as the Minangkabau culture of West Sumatra, the Ezhavea, Nairs and Kurichiyas of Kerala, India, Bunts, Billavas and Mogaveeras of Karnatake, Pillai caste in Nagercoiil District of Tamil Nadu, the Khasi and Garo of Meghalaya, India, the Naxi of China, the Gitksan of British Colombia, the Iroquois Confederacy (Haudenosaunee), the Hopi and the Tuaregs.

In the ancient kingdom of Ellan, the succession to the throne was matrilineal and a nephew would succeed his maternal uncle to the throne.

The order of succession to the position of the Rain Queen is a modern example in an African culture of matrilineal progeniture: not only is dynastic descent reckoned through the female line, but only females, not males are eligible to inherit.

1. GENETIC GENEALOGY

The fact that mitochondrial (mtDNA) is maternally inherited enables matrilineal lines of individuals to be traced through genetic analysis. Mitochondrial Eve (mtmrca) is the name given by researchers to the woman who is the matrilineal most recent common ancestor for all living humans, from whom all mtDNA in living humans is derived. She is believed by some to have lived about 150,000 years ago in what is now Ethiopia, Kenya or Tanzania. The time she lived is calculated based on the molecular clock technique of correlating elapsed time with observed genetic drift.

All of a woman's children (both boys and girls) normally inherit their mt-DNA from the mother and it consequently comes from their mother's mother, and so on, upon along the family tree in exclusive matrilineal. As mt-DNA is sort of "cellular power plants," one's metabolism and energy conversion are much influenced by the matrilineal descent.

Already ancient physicians had an inkling about matrilineal heredity. A child's physical frame will mostly be provided by maternal heredity.

Attempts have been made to trace fatness and slimness along matrilines in genealogies of persons whose physical details are well-archived, such as the royally stout Queen Victoria of the United Kingdom.

There has been a hypothesis that better and worse suitability to give birth would be a maternally hereditary physical characteristic. If so, unsuitable matrilines are highly prone to extinction, whereas suitable matrilines would prosper.

Clearly, you can see that for the Kono, the existence of life is determined by the Mother's "breast Milk".

Therefore, any act that violates this mother concept is deemed a taboo the Damby. ***This is understood that all children were first fed on the mother's breast milk, the first human food shared by males and female of a mother.***

Therefore, all children that shared or fed on a mother's breast are considered siblings for the sake of establishing laws against incest. Since the siblings shared a common DNA from the mother, they are deemed ***genetically*** unfit to have sexual relationships or for inter marriages.

Since the Damby Concept seems to parallel the concept of "genetic Engineering", I will ask your indulgence to examine the concept of cell Engineering in some detailed below.

SECTION I
SPECIAL SECTION
FOR CLARITY

CHAPTER TWO

Lamina, [Lam·i·na (Lam·i·nae, or Lam·i·nas)] [Lam·i·na [Lámmənə] (Plural [Lámmənee])

The word Lamina is an African and it is a birth given name for males. In the Kono tradition it is an initiation names chosen or given to Kono males who have been initiated into to the Poro or Poneh for males only. One such male was my uncle Lamin of Bayamah, Gbenseh chiefdom. He was one of the highest ranking elders of the Trade.

However, For The Purpose Of This Book, The Word "Lamina" Is Defined As A Thin Layer, A Thin Plate Or Flake; And Since We Are Talking About The Damby Food Or Diet Prohibitions A BotAnic Definition Is Therefore, A Must.

In *botany* the word lamina means, the blade or flat part of a leaf. Also, since we are talking about the Damby prohibitions which are mostly animals, a zoological definition is also a must. Thus, in *Zoology* the word Lamina means, protective plate in hoofed mammals; and also means any of the parallel layers of sensitive tissues just inside the hard exterior of the hoof. With this said, will now discuss the rest of the proteins' functions below.

The *basement membrane* is the sheets of protein that form the substrate of all internal organs. It is the major non-collagenous: the main protien of connetive tissues in animals and the most abundant protein in mammals, making up about 25% to 35% of the whole-body protein content.

Laminin, component of the basal *lamina*, such as those on which cells of an epthuelium sit. It has ***four arms*** that can bind to four other molecules. The three shorter arms are particularly good at bibding to other *laminin* molecules, and this is what makes it significant in forming sheets. The long arm is capable of binding to cells, this helps it anchor the actual organs to the membrane. *(Do you still wonder why there were 4 females at 'sideof Jesus on the day of his cruxifiction each call Marry?)*

The laminin protein is made up of three separate parts, called the A, B1, and B2 chains. (does the Christian concept of the trinity ring a bell) These give it a total of **six** "ends" (*note, the concept of the star of Davud or the hexegram*), which accounts for a lot of its flexibility in connecting to various kinds of molecules. Because of this, scientists who create biomaterials are extremely interested in the whole family of laminins. They are a family of gycoprotein that are an integral part of the structural scaffolding in almost every animal tissue. Laminins are secreted and incorporated into cell-associated extracellar matrices.

Laminin is vital to making sure overall body structures hold together. Improper production of laminin can cause muscles to form improperly, leading to a form of muscular dystrphy. It can also cause *progeria*.

The biological information contained in an organism is encoded in its DNA or RNA sequence. RNA is also used for information transport for example, the mRNA and the enzymatic functions the ribonsomal RNA) in organisms that use DNA for the genetic code itself. Transfer RNA (tRNA) molecules are used to add specific amino acids during the process of protein translation.

A human cell has genetic material in the nucleus; also known as the **nuclear genome)** and and in the mitochondria: **the mitrochondrial genome**. Note here that the word Gina is a name given to afemale of a sinlge birth immediately after the birth of twins or other multiple births, the name means "spirit" and it is derived from the word *genome*. *Nynnah or gynnah* are Mande or Kono word for spirit.

In humans the nuclear genome is divided into 23 pairs of linear DNA molecules called chromosomes. The **mitochondrial genome is a circular** (*like the roundness of a pregnant belly*) DNA molecule is distinct from the nuclear DNA. Note here also that the 25 paired human genme sum up to 46 genomes. Now, here comes the genuis of the ancient Kono. Remember that one of the Damby totemic groups is called "San-du-u", the ancient meaning of this word is "five-moons" and for a good reason.

The 23 paired genomes is actually 2 + 3=5 genomes + 2 + 3 = 5 genomes; now, 5 + 5 = 10 then 1 + 0 = "0" or zero, Zero, you know can be represented by a "." Or "dot"; we have all heard of the word "Dot logic". Another name for dot is "Spot". The Leopard is one the animals in the animal king known for its *spoted skin.* therefore, the ancient man compared the spots of the Leopard to the night sky spotted by the stars.

The ancient Kono were astrologers, thus they knew number as well as letter values. Therefore, they reasoned, 23 paired genome or spirits in humans eguals "10", which for them was a number depicting God, And, since 10 represents 1 and 0 or Alpha and Omega, then, 1 = A while 0 is Omega. The "San-du-u", the Leopad totemic Damby means five moons as already stated, 'San', 'Sand', 'Sinn' or 'Sinnah', are various ancient names for the Moon. These names are also the Bibliacal names for the moon in the Old Testament: Sin, Zin, and when the name "On", the center the moon worship was added to Sin or Zin i. e., Sin-On, Zin-On the ancient came up with name Sion or Zion, Thus, in the Old Testament of the Bible father Abram was called Abrham of On written as Hur.

In the Sandur Chiefdom, note the name Sandur to be **Sand-On or Sand-Ur.** This simple reference to the moon gives the bases for understanding the Leopard Priests of ancient Egypt as well as the bases for ancient cultural rulers wore Leopard skins.

Before we move on remember the name Sand or San means the moon, thus another meaning of the world **Sanduu** means 5 moon cycles and threfore depicts "Blood" issues because the moon governs the blood.

Although the **mitochondrial DNA** is very small compared to nuclear chromosomes, it codes for **13 proteins** involved in mitochondrial energy production as well as specific tRNAs.

Note here that the number 13 is the number of months in a Luna (Moon) year, this correspnds to the menstrual cycle of menstruation females. Hence the coagulated menstrual blood manifest as a baby or child.

Foreign genetic material (most commonly DNA) can also be artificially introduced into the cell by a process called transfection (creation from a genetic Labs). This can be transient, if the DNA is not inserted into the cell's genome, or s if it is table, certain viruses can also insert their genetic material into the genome.

ORGANELLES

The human body contains many different organs, such as the heart, lung, and kidney, with each organ performing a different function.

LITTLE ORGANS

Cells also have a set of "little organs," called organelles that are adapted and/or specialized for carrying out one or more vital functions. Also, note here that the word *yu-u-kanneh* and the word organelle parallel each other. Now, since the *yu-ukanneh* is a feminine tool used in Kono females' secret society, there must have been an etymological connection between both words. Furthermore, the mitochondrial DNA like the *yu-u-kanneh* is exclusively a feminine thing.

There are several types of organelles within an animal cell. Some (such as the nucleus, and golgi (Konkai) apparatus are typically solitary, while others (such as mitochondrial, peroisomes and lysosomes,) can be numerous (hundreds to thousands). The cytosol is the gelatinous fluid that fills the cell and surrounds the organelles.

Golgi apparatus is a structure in cytoplasm: a membranous structure in the cytoplasm of cells consisting of layers of flattened sacs and functioning in the processing and transporting of proteins. Do not flattened saclike tailed sperm cells carry chemical substances to waiting egg that results in conception? This is why the Kono name for this structure is 'Kon-Kai', meaning, broken down tree, or tree breaker. Therefore, in the Kono tradition one will find males called Konkai or Konkaiwah.

CHAPTER THREE

Mitochondria and Chloroplasts (The Power Generators)

Mitochondrial are self-replicating organelles that occur in various numbers, shapes, and sizes in the cytoplasm of all eukaryotic cells. Mitochondria play a critical role in generating energy in the eukaryotic cell.

RIBOSOMES

The Ribonsome is a large complex of RNA and protein molecules. This is where proteins are produced. Ribosomes can be found either foating freely or bound to a membrane (the rough endoplasmatic reticulum in eukaryotes, or the cell membrane in prokaryotes).

Eukaryotic cells are about 10 times the size of a typical prokaryote and can be as much as 1000 times greater in volume. The major difference between prokaryotes and eukaryotes is that eukaryotic cells contain membrane-bound compartments in which specific metabolic activities take place. Most important among these is the presence of a cell nucleus, a membrane-delineated compartment that houses the eukaryotic cell's DNA. It is this nucleus that gives the eukaryote its name, which means "***true nucleus***." Other differences include:

The plasma membrane resembles that of prokaryotes in function, with minor differences in the setup. Cell walls may or may not be present.

The eukaryotic DNA is organized in one or more linear molecules, called chromosomes, which are associated with histone proteins. All chromosomal DNA is stored in the cell nucleus, separated from the cytoplasm by a membrane. Some eukaryotic organelles such as mitochondria also contain some DNA.

Eukaryotes can move using *cilia* or *flagella*. The flagella are more complex than those of prokaryotes.

CELL NUCLEUS (A CELL'S INFORMATION CENTER)

The cell nucleus is the most conspicuous organelle found in a eukaryotic [like rope] cell. It houses the cell's chromosomes, [komo] and is the place where almost all DNA replication and RNA synthesis (transcription) occur. The nucleus is spherical in shape and separated from the cytoplasm by a double membrane called the *nuclear envelope*. The nuclear envelope isolates and protects a cell's DNA from various molecules that could accidentally damage its structure or interfere with its processing. During processing, DNA is transcribed, or copied into a special RNA, called mRNA. This mRNA is then transported out of the nucleus, where it is translated into a specific protein molecule. The nucleolus is a specialized region within the nucleus where ribosome subunits are assembled. In prokaryotes, DNA processing takes place in the cytoplasm.

CELL GROWTH AND METABOLISM

Between successive cell divisions, cells grow through the functioning of cellular metabolism.

Cell metabolism is the process by which individual cells process nutrient molecules. Metabolism has two distinct divisions: catabolism, in which the cell breaks down complex molecules to produce energy and reducing power, and anabolism, in which the cell uses energy and reducing power to construct complex molecules and perform other biological functions. Complex sugars consumed by the organism can be broken down into a less chemically-complex sugar molecule called glucose. Once inside the cell, glucose is broken down to make adenosine triphosphate (ATP) a form of energy, via two different pathways.

The first pathway, glycolysis, requires no oxygen and is referred to as anaerobic metabolism. Each reaction is designed to produce some hydrogen ions that can then be used to make energy packets (ATP). In prokaryotes, glycolysis is the only method used for converting energy.

The second pathway, called the Krebs cycle, or citric acid cycle, occurs inside the mitochondria and is capable of generating enough ATP to run all the cell functions.

An overview of protein synthesis.

Within the nucleus of the cell genes DNA, are transcribed into RNA. This RNA is then subject to post-transcriptional modification and control, resulting in a mature mRNA that is then transported out of the nucleus and into the cytoplasm where it undergoes translation into a protein. mRNA is translated by ribosomes that match the three-base codons of the mRNA to the three-base anti-codons of the appropriate tRNA. Newly-synthesized proteins are often further modified, such as by binding to an effector molecule to become fully active. [Notes **Codons** *are the basic unit of genetic code: a unit in messenger RNA consisting of a set of three consecutive nucleotides that specifies a particular amino acid in protein synthesis*]

CREATION OF NEW CELLS OR *CELL DIVISION*

Cell division involves a single cell (called a *mother cell*) dividing into two daughter cells. This leads to growth in multicultural organisms (the growth of tissue) and to procreation (vegetative reproduction) in unicellular organisms.

Followed by division of the cell, called cytokines is. A diploid cell may also undergo meiosis to produce haploid cells, usually four. Haploid cells serve as gametes in multicellular organisms, fusing to form new diploid cells.

DNA replication, or the process of duplicating a cell's genome, is required every time a cell divides. Replication, like all cellular activities, requires specialized proteins for carrying out the job.

PROTEIN SYNTHESIS

Cells are capable of synthesizing new proteins, which are essential for the modulation and maintenance of cellular activities. This process involves the formation of new protein molecules from amino acid building blocks based on information encoded in DNA/RNA. Protein synthesis generally consists of two major steps: transcription and translation.

Transcription is the process where genetic information in DNA is used to produce a complementary RNA strand. This RNA strand is then processed to give messenger RNA (mRNA) (mRNA), which is free to migrate through the cell. mRNA molecules bind to protein-RNA complexes called ribosome located in the cytosol, where they are translated into polypeptide sequences. The ribosome mediates the formation of a polypeptide sequence based on the mRNA sequence. The mRNA sequence directly relates to the polypeptide sequence by binding to transfer RNA (tRNA) (tRNA) adapter molecules in binding pockets within the ribosome. The new polypeptide then folds into a functional three-dimensional protein molecule.

A *chromosome* is an organized structure of DNA and protein that is found in cells. A chromosome is a single piece of DNA that contains many genes, regulatory elements and other nucleotide sequences. Chromosomes also contain DNA-bound proteins, which serve to package the DNA and control its functions. The word *chromosome* comes from the Greek χρ🔲μα (*chroma*, color, the word 'chroma is derived from the Kono word Komane or *Komanenu*, people whose totemic animal is the viper, even in modern times we believe there is a relationship between the word snake and the blood, and this is due to the structures of some components of the blood; and σ🔲μα (*soma*, body) due to their property of being stained very strongly by some dyes.

Chromosomes vary extensively between different organism. Also, the word chromosome has a parallel to the following Kono words, *Komo*, an initiation name for Kono females, thus the word Komo-Musu, meaning Komo female interprets to mean an exceptional woman, one such woman was my step-great grand mother, Komo. Grand mother of my step mother Finda Madiana. Granny Komo was one of those luck females who managed to escape the slave ships destined for North America before the ships sailed during the colonial-slaving days of the African people. Komo was able to return home and married one of the local chiefs.

HUMAN MITOCHONDRIAL GENETICS

As explained above human mitochondrial genetics is the study of the genetics of the DNA contained in human mitochondria. Mitochondria are small structures in cells that generate energy for the cell to use, and are hence referred to as the "powerhouses" of the cell.

Mitochondrial DNA (mtDNA) is not transmitted through nuclear DNA (nDNA), and in most multicellular organisms, *virtually all mitochondria are inherited from the mother's ovum, as it is unusual for sperm cells to contribute mitochondria when fertilising ova.* Mitochondrial inheritance is therefore non-Mendelian, as Mendelian inheritance presumes that half the genetic material of a fertilized egg (zygote) derives from each parent.

Eighty percent of mitochondrial DNA codes for functional mitochondrial proteins, and therefore most mitochondrial DNA mutations lead to functional problems, which may be manifested as muscle disorders (myopathies).

- Understanding the genetic mutations that affect mitochondria can help us to understand the inner workings of cells and organisms, as well as helping to suggest methods for successful therapeutic tissue and organ cloning, and to treatments or possibly cures for many devastating as the first base of the next gene.

GENETICS

Genetics (from Ancient Greek γενετικός *genetikos*, "genitive" and that from γένεσις *genesis*, "origin"), a discipline of biology, is the science of heredity and variation in living organisms. The fact that living things inherit traits from their parents has been used since prehistoric times to improve crop plants and animals through selective breeding. However, the modern science of genetics, which seeks to understand the process of inheritance, only began with the work of Gregor Mendel in the mid-nineteenth century. Although he did not know the physical basis for heredity, Mendel observed that organisms inherit traits in a discrete manner—these basic units of inheritance are now called genes.

DNA, the molecular basis for inheritance. Each strand of DNA is a chain of <u>nucleotides</u>, matching each other in the center to form what look like rungs on a twisted ladder.

Genes correspond to regions within DNA, a molecule composed of a chain of four different types of nucleotides—the sequence of these nucleotides is the genetic information organisms inherit. DNA naturally occurs in a double stranded form, with nucleotides on each strand complementary to each other. Each strand can act as a template for creating a new partner strand—this is the physical method for making copies of genes that can be inherited.

The sequence of nucleotides in a gene is translated by cells to produce a chain of amino acids, creating proteins—the order of amino acids in a protein corresponds to the order of nucleotides in the gene. This is known as the genetic code. The amino acids in a protein determine how it folds into a three-dimensional shape; this structure is, in turn, responsible for the protein's function.

PROTEIN'S FUNCTION

Proteins carry out almost all the functions needed for cells to live. A change to the DNA in a gene can change a protein's amino acids, changing its shape and function: this can have a dramatic effect in the cell and on the organism as a whole.

Although genetics plays a large role in the appearance and behavior of organisms, it is the combination of genetics with what an organism experiences that determines the ultimate outcome. For example, while genes play a role in determining a person's height, the nutrition and health that person experiences in childhood also have a large effect.

DAMBY RESEARCH PROJECT

Population genetics research studies the distributions of these genetic differences within populations and how the distributions change over time. Changes in the frequency of an allele in a population can be influenced by natural selection, where a given allele's higher rate of survival and reproduction causes it to become more frequent in the population over time. Genetic drift can also occur, where chance events lead to random changes in allele frequency. Over many generations, the genomes of organisms can change, resulting in the phenomenon of evolution.

Mutations and the selection for beneficial mutations can cause a species to evolve into forms that better survive their environment, a process called adaptation. New species are formed through the process of speciation, a process often caused by geographical separations that allow different populations to genetically diverge The application of genetic principles to the study of population biology and evolution is referred to as the modern synthesis.

As sequences diverge and change during the process of evolution, these differences between sequences can be used as a molecular clock to calculate the evolutionary distance between them. Genetic comparisons are generally considered the most accurate method of characterizing the relatedness between species, an improvement over the sometimes deceptive comparison of phenotypic characteristics.

The evolutionary distances between species can be combined to form evolutionary trees—these trees represent the common descent and divergence of species over time, although they cannot and most common in bacteria). The Damby System can represent the transfer of genetic material between unrelated species (known as horizontal gene transfer represent the transfer of genetic material between unrelated species (known as horizontal gene transfer

MEDICAL GENETICS RESEARCH

Medical genetics seeks to understand how genetic variation relates to human health and disease. When searching for an unknown gene that may be involved in a disease, researchers commonly use genetic linkage and genetic pedigree charts to find the location on the genome associated with the disease. At the population level, researchers take advantage of Mendelian randomization to look for locations in the genome that are associated with diseases, a technique especially useful for multigenic traits not clearly defined by a single gene. Once a candidate gene is found, further research is often done on the same gene (called an orthologous gene) in model organisms. In addition to studying genetic diseases, the increased availability of genotyping techniques has led to the field of pharmacogenetics—studying how genotype can affect drug responses.

DAMBI GENETICS POSSIBILITIES

DNA can be manipulated in the laboratory. Restriction enzymes are a commonly used enzyme that cuts DNA at specific sequences, producing predictable fragments of DNA. The use of ligation enzymes allows these fragments to be reconnected, and by ligating fragments of DNA together from different sources, researchers can create recombinant DNA. Often associated with genetically modified organisms, recombinant DNA is commonly used in the context of plasmids—short circular DNA fragments with a few genes on them. By inserting plasmids into bacteria and growing those bacteria on plates of agar (to isolate clones of bacteria cells), researchers can clonally amplify the inserted fragment of DNA (a process known as molecular cloning). (Cloning can also refer to the creation of clonal organisms, through various techniques.)

DNA can also be amplified using a procedure called the polymerase chain reaction (PCR). By using specific short sequences of DNA, PCR can isolate and exponentially amplify a targeted region of DNA. Because it can amplify from extremely small amounts of DNA, PCR is also often used to detect the presence of specific DNA sequences.

DAMBY DNA SEQUENCING AND GENOMICS VIA THE USE OF COMPUTERS

One of the most fundamental technologies developed to study genetics, DNA sequencing allows researchers to determine the sequence of nucleotides in DNA fragments. Developed in 1977 by Frederick Sanger and coworkers, chain-termination sequencing is now routinely used to sequence DNA fragments. With this technology, researchers have been able to study the molecular sequences associated with many human diseases.

As sequencing has become less expensive and with the aid of computational tools, researchers can sequenced the genomes of many all members by stitching together the sequences of many different fragments (a process called genome assembly).

These technologies were used to sequence the human genome, leading to the completion of the Human Genome Project in 2003. New high-throughput sequencing technologies are dramatically lowering the cost of DNA sequencing, with many researchers hoping to bring the cost of resequencing a human genome down to a thousand dollars. The large amount of sequences available has created the field of genomics, research that uses computational tools to search for and analyze patterns in the full genomes of organisms. Genomics can also be considered a subfield of bioinformatics, which uses computational approaches to analyze large sets of biological data.

CHAPTER FOUR

Laminin:

In chapter one above I explained the meaning of the word Lamina from the Kono or African perspectives. In the explanations, I maintained that the name Lamin is an initiation name in the Kono tradition. In this chapter, I will establish why the word Laminin is an initiation name for males in the Kono tradition. The word Laminin has many variations, i. e., Lamin, Lamina, Damie, or Damina depending on which area one is from. Since the name is an initiation name, it must therefore, have a secret meaning. In addition, since the word Lamin or Lamina parallels the word Damby, its secret meaning must be related to a "blood" or a "blood-line' issues.

Let me explain:
The word Lamina is exactly what the ancient Kono had in mind when he coined the word *"Sun-yu-u", "Sun-gu-u" or "Swoon-yu" or "Swoon-gu-u"*.

LAMININ, NOW KNOWN AS THE "CROSS" PROTEIN

As already explained elsewhere in the chapters of this book, the word "Sun-yu-u", "Sun-gu-u" or "Swoon-yu" or "Swoon-gu-u" in the kono tradition means basically "blood lines", or "Damby", the cord, chain string or rope that binds: to hold individuals together in a family unit that goes way back to pre-historic times. This is a kono swoon-yu-uu or family cords.

According to studies in Cell biology, The word Laminin is presents as a protein substance found in the extracellular matrix, of a cell. It functions to provide structural support to the animal cells. Laminin is a protein found on the outer part of cells: commonly known as the extracellular matrix. Laminin is also found in tissues that provide structural support to the cells as well as performing other important functions.

FORMATION

Laminin molecules are formed by joining together to form sheets of protein that are the basic cellular source of all internal organs. Laminin as molecules basically comes in what is known as *'short and long arms'* that bind to other Laminin molecules, such as the short arms bind well to form the sheets of membranes, and the long arms bind to cells that help to anchor the organs to the sheet membranes.

The Laminin protein molecule demonstrate to us what the ancient Mystery Schools maintained, that the number three or the triangles are sacred numbers that depict the power of God or God Himself depending on the school of thought you agree with.

This is the basis of the Christian explanation of the Trinity. The Kono basis for the names of the Triple Rivers: Baffin, Bagheh, and Bayawah or Bayah; and the *Triple Naming tradition* of female *triplets* in the *Kono Onomastics: Sokoh, Femusu and Digbah*. It was also the basis of the ancient *Egyptian triple gods, Horus, Seth and Osiris*. Furthermore, *it is the basis for believe in the triple stars of the Sirius system: Sirius A, B, and C.* furthermore, it is the basis for all *cultural believe in the power of the number three.*

The reason for this is found in the fact that Laminin Proteins are formed by **three** *separate chains called* **A, B-1, and B-2 chains that form six ends** that help the Laminin sheets to bind when attaching to various kinds of molecules in the body. Therefore, Laminin is vital to making sure that all body structures hold together securely, other wise, various muscle and tissue diseases result.

As stated above, Kono Tradition basically called the number three, **"Sawah",** meaning the *'Law'*. This interprets to mean that the Universe is governed by laws beyond our control and understanding.

In addition, the Kono call the *number 6 'wau'*, this word in the ancient Greek's numbering system where 6 is represented by the symbol for the obsolete letter *digamma*. digamma □, (also used are stigma □ or, in modern Greek, στ) for 6

Gamma, on the other hand is *number 3*. The *number 3 or* gamma is affirmed in the word Digamma, also called 'Wau' or "Vau", Digamma (DI means 2) means two gammas this equals to digamma, Wau or the number 6 contains two numbers represented in the so-called star of David, which is echoed in the Kono word for the number 7. In the Kono language, the number seven or "7" is called **'Wau-faiyah'** meaning twice "Wau". Twice Wau is 2 x Wau or 2 x 6 = 12=1 + 2 = 3 = Digamma. These explanations are supported by the image of the triple Laminin Proteins: A, B1 and B2. So here is what the Laminin molecule looks like. (Link top of Page)

The Laminin Proteins controversy has given an edge to the Christian *Trinity Concept and it is using the Holy Bible's Book of Colossians* to support its claim. For example, **Colossians 1: 15-17** states: *"He is the image of the invisible God, the first born over all creation. For by Him all things were created; things in heaven and on earth, visible and invisible, whether thrones or powers or rulers or authorities; all things were created by Him and for Him. He is before all things, and in Him all things hold together."*

However, if this is what we need to accept the Christian god then all cultural gods are creator gods in their own rights; for all cultural religions claim that only their creator god could have known what the bonding molecule of our bodies would look like long before He created *in his or her image and likeness.*

Ecclesiastes 4:12b it says *". . . a three fold cord is not quickly broken."* Funny how the Kono words: AU, U-Uu, WAU, are expressing the letter *'U'* or *'YU-U'* which depicts **the thread, rope, cord or string**, usually derived from the bamboo canes (*simine*, note the parallel between the words simine and lamina), and *gnomoe*h (note the parallel between the words genome and gnomeh. Kono tradition *"Siminegie*, obviously derived from the word simine is a name given to females i.e., my aunt's name. The word simineh is a Kono word for the bamboo cane. The word *'Uu'* or *'yu-u'* the **mystical rope, thread. String or cord** that binds things together and is found in the names of ancient Egyptian Horus (HOR-R-US) and in the Christian Jesus (JE-S-US) in the form of the letter "U" is the Kono basis for the concept of the *"Suun-yu-u"* or *"Swoon-yu-u"*.

The word lamin, is obviously derived from the word Laminin a Kono word or name give to a male i. e., my uncle's. *". . . you are My Son today I have begotten you*?" . . . See **Heb. 1:5**-13.

In addition, it is my opinion that the words Lamin or Laminin and Damby have the same etymology. The Kono Damby Tradition is essentially dealing with blood and its components issues, 90% of the Damby prohibitions are foods sources high in proteins.

Laminin is designed in three fold types of structure that acts like a sort of glue-like, string, rope or cord that hold us together by tying the cells in specific shapes and forms for functional purposes.

Colossians 1:17-20, 22, 26-29 says: *"And he (Christ) is before all things, and in HIM all things consist."* and in **verse 20** we read *". . . have made peace through the **blood** of his **cross** KJV. **Verse 26** ". . . the mystery which has been hidden from ages and from generations but now has bee revealed to his saints. **Verse 27** ". . . this mystery among gentiles which is christ in you, the hope of glory."*

In short, the Laminin is a cell *adhesion* protein molecule. It's like a tiny, weeny molecule that glues our bodies together. Therefore, if we accept this notion and we are christians then, we are like cells in the body and "Christ" is the "Laminin" of our being.

Haw! No wonder my father once said that, *"we the Kono know Jesus the Christ more than those who profess to be our teachers of him"*. I always knew there was something special about my uncle Lamine. However, because the Kono language depending on which chiefdom one is from, does not have an "L" sound, thus, some people call him **"Damine"**.

How can a protein that holds the cells together be interpreted to mean the very symbol of or the Christian Savior who delivered us from all sins, pains and doubts?

Nonetheless, true or false, the Christian preacher, Louie Giglio is selling the images of the laminin protein from a microscopic slide he claimed to have been sent to him from a molecular biologist who introduced him to laminin as the very emblem of the christian cross. However, those scientist are still ignoring the facts that the ancient Egyptians (Africans) have said the same thing *of the Southern Cross* depicted on the robes of catholic popes and priests. As a matter of fact the *cross was known as the pigmy Tau*. The ancient Kono call this cross *Tambaa and Kombaa, (the Arrow and the Mighty Tree).*

LAMININ Vs. THE KONO FEMALE'S WU-KANEH

Laminin is a protein in our body that literally holds our skin, organs, and everything else in our body, in place. It was described as the rebar of the human. **Laminin . . .** it holds us all together. This definition is what is depicted in the Kono female's *Wu-kaneh* in a form of a circle depicting the cell and all its possibilities. See pictures below of the Laminin protein.

See picture on the top left, Wu-Kaneh or Yuu-kaneh: is shown, front role in the hands of the 3rd girl from left to right, also note that the 2nd and 4th girls are holding fish-nets, another emblem of the Sandaih (the fishing net is also associated with Jesus, but now we know that the Kono tradition had it before the Jesus' mission), these 4 Kono females are on their way to becoming *Sandaih Musu*, (Sandaih women) . . .

Among some Christians, numerous icons and symbols, such as: crosses, fishes, crucifixes, statues, medallions, figurines, candle sticks, etc are used in the rituals. But no one would ascribe fetish powers to these Christian icons and symbols. Nonetheless, one must understand that in West African cultures, unlike Christian icons and symbols, behind the fetish is the religion of the worship of the 'mind' of our ancestors and the fetish is better understood as a religious symbol. Ancestor worship is also part of the African's strong family ties (the swoon-yu-u or Lamin/Damin) and its powerful kinship, or Damby patterns.

Besides the above-mentioned sources of African history, oral tradition takes its place as a real living museum—a conserver and transmitter of the social and cultural creations stored up by peoples said to have no written records. This spoken history is a very *frail thread* that can be used to trace our way back through the dark twists and turns in the labyrinth of time. Those who are its custodians are hoary-headed old men and women with cracking voices, often dim memories, and a stickler's insistence on etiquette that behooves potential ancestors. They are like the last remaining inlets in a landscape that was once imposing and coherent, but which is now eroded, flattened, and thrown into disorder by the sharp waves of modernism. (One such old man was my father.)

SECTION II

CHAPTER FIVE

What Breaks the Lamini or Swoon-Yu-U Ties?

1, LEGAL IMPLICATIONS
2, INCESTIOUS BEHAVIOURS
3, VIOLATIONS OF DAMBY EXPECTATIONS

The break up of 'swoon-yu-u' and therefore the Damby chain or Bloodline as stated above and aught to be repeated here are the following:

INCEST PROHIBITION IN THE DAMBY TRADITION

The Kono Tradition Kono offers no exception to the fact that the starting point of the family organization is the union of the male and female in marriage. Kono social tradition gives rise to certain marriage covenant terms, here called LAWS, which govern the formation of kin groups as well as the relationship between men and women in a Kono society. Some of the more important covenant terms are described below.

These laws are what distinguished the Kono from other Mande speaking people. While as cross-marriages are prohibited among the Kono in this Era, words such as **(mbia—musu, mbia-gai. N'nii-moe, m'bain, dain-na-musu, tain-sa-musu, tain-sa-kai and mba or Ba)** are an implication pointing to ancient cross-marriages before the Great Mande People before they broke up into what is now handed down to us as tribes. This oral tradition has embedded in it legal implications, and these traditions are still prevalent in today's Kono society.

Marriage within same Kono Damby or clan is prohibited. All marriages have to be sought outside the clan. This is called Damby or clan exogamy. Clan organization has been described in detail. Through a single-descendant patrilineal family, the Kono are able to preserve the unity of the clan groups mainly through clan exogamy.

LAW OF SUMO-GAI-MA (A KONO WORD FOR INCEST) OR TABOO REGULATIONS REGARDING MARRIAGE

According to their tradition, brothers and sisters have a **Sumo-gai-ma" (taboo sexual)** relationship and no marriage or sex is allowed between them. This kind of brother-sister relationship is extended to collateral branches to include fathers brothers sons and daughters and eventually all the males and females of the same generation [who are descended from males] within the patrilineal clan, all of whom are strictly prohibited to intermarry.

Within the Kono family, brothers and sisters both grow up under parental protection. Their relationship is affectionate but formal, and licentious behavior between them is absolutely forbidden. Although love affairs are quit common among the Kono a brother should not flirt with a girl in the presence of her brother; otherwise her brother would beat him, and their quarrel, once stirred up, might lead to a clan feud (**Soo-don-do-e**). Male and female members of the same clan, between whom marriage is prohibited because of age-old traditions, usually behave toward each other in accordance with a formal code of propriety.

THE IDEAL MARRIAGE PARTNER IS ONE'S CROSS-COUSIN

Since it seems the Kono formally have to select their mates from within the same class but outside the clan, what kind of family group is the best from which to seek an ideal mate? According to The Ancient Kono tradition, the ideal marriage partner is ones cross-cousin; hence there are numerous cases of cross-cousin marriage, still being practiced among the Mandinkas and other Mande speakers.

In these Mande families that still practice the 'Old-ways', if a girl's paternal aunt has a male and the male's maternal uncle is the father of the girl, then the boy's family has priority in sending a match-maker to negotiate for the girl's hand. For this reason the maternal uncle dare not marry his daughter into another family. Likewise, the son of a girl's maternal uncle has the same priority over her, a daughter of his paternal aunt. Therefore, there is a mutual marriage relationship between the sons and daughters of the two families. One can find many evidences of this form of cross-cousin marriages even now from Kono kinship terms. The terms used to establish relationship points to cross-cousin marriages. These terms have being isolated and would be fully explained in the Notes below. The terms associated with marriage seem to suggest that the Kono must have had similar marriage customs.

The Mandinka for instant, when they were not known as Kono people must have practiced other forms of marriages. It is the form of marriages that we are going to **explore.** *Tain-sa-musu, tain-sa-kai, nii-mor-moe, bia-musu, bia-gai. Dai-moe, and dain-na-musu* are some of such terms that indicated very close blood ties. Because of his marriage to maternal uncle's daughter, the boy also calls his father-in-law maternal uncle and his mother-in-law maternal uncle's wife. Hence the son-in-law is also the sister's son. On the other hand, because of her marriage to the son of her paternal aunt's family, the girl calls her husbands mother paternal aunt and her husband's father paternal aunt's husband.

CROSS-COUSIN MARRIAGE

Cross-cousin marriage is not unilateral, but multilateral in terms of relationships. The son also sometimes marries the daughter of the paternal aunt; therefore, he calls his mother-in-law, paternal aunt and his father-in-law paternal aunt's husband. In this case, the son-in-law is also the wife's brother's son. The girl is sometimes married the son of the maternal uncle; therefore she calls her husband's parents maternal uncle and maternal uncle's wife. In that case the daughter-in-law is the husband's sister's daughter.

SPECIAL KINSHIP TERMS OF ADDRESS BETWEEN WIFE'S PARENTS

Since it seems the Kono have practiced cross-cousin marriage for generations, there are special kinship terms of address between wife's parents [(bia-musu for wife's mother and bia-gai, wife's older male relatives including the father, and nii-moe for both younger male and female relatives, and son-in-law(biaa-gai, whether old or young)], and between father-in-law and daughter-in-law[dain-na-musu] are bifurcated from the wife's clan, which in which in turn is bifurcated from the mother's clan. Since the Kono seem to put great value on male gender this may explain the maternal uncles (bain-du-moe-nu are so important in all Kono children's lives. The relationship between the patrilineal and matrilineal clans is the closest as they are continuously interlinked through marriage.

The Konos have turned away from cross marriages; however, their cousins Mandingos still retain this custom, as described above.

Because of their priority in marriage, Kono cross-cousins treat each other quite differently from the way brothers and sisters treat each other. Cross-cousins of the opposite sex who have preferential marriage privileges can play and flirt with each other and eventually have sexual relationship after marriage. This is quite different from the strict relationship between brother and sisters, who never act loosely toward each other. Therefore, it can be seen how customs and traditions mold individual behavior and attitudes and how they regulate interpersonal obligations and duties.

KONO PREFERENTIAL MARRIAGE

Kono preferential marriage is limited to cross-cousins, including one and fathers sisters daughter or one's and mother's brother's daughter, mothers sister's daughter and one are also prohibited from contracting marriage relationships. This prohibition of maternal parallel-cousin marriage is quit different from the **Mandika**) custom and may be due to the Kono emphasis on the maternal lineage. The children of the maternal aunt are treated in the same way as the children of the paternal uncle. In the Kono language, mother's sisters children are also addressed as (**N'dai-su-neh-nu**), denoting a relationship similar to that between brothers and sisters. Therefore they are accorded the same treatment.

N'TAIN-SA

N'TAIN-SA, MEANING non-sexual blood relative is another world used to address kin members who are sisters and brothers from the some parents. As a matter of fact, the lack of population growth and the high mortality rate among the Kono makes it exceedingly rare to have more than nine brothers in a family, unless it is a polygamous family type, where a man can marry as many wives as he can support . . . The children of father's elder brothers are all called elder brothers and sisters in their age order, even though some of them may be younger than ego. On the other hand, the children of father's younger brothers, whatever their age, are called by their names.

SU-MA-NYUE-NU AND M'BA-A-CHAIN-NE-NU

Cross cousins and parallel cousins are two appositive cousins; and so are children of elder and younger sisters, although they differ in Kono terms. Children of elder brother and younger sister of those of elder sister and younger brother are all cross cousins, for which there is in the Kono language a collective term, (**su-ma-nyue-nu**). This is in opposition to the term (m'ba-**a-chain-ne-nu**), and the relationships they refer to are also opposite. In the former relationship, cross cousins have preferential marriage privileges, whereas in the later, all brothers and sisters as well as parallel cousins are for bidden to intermarry.

CHAPTER SIX

Purification Process for Violations of Damby Expectations

There are two main forms of purification process that are officiated only by the Gbain-gain-ne-nu, a group within the *Sumoeh*, a *Sandur Chiefdom Mystic Secret Society* whose Queen of the group is **Bor-Gbin**, meaning ". . . a seated Mighty Mother".

TWO MAIN FORMS OF PURIFICATION PROCESS

1) OWO-A-TE-EH

This process involves the Cutting down of a ko-nut tree branch. The reason for this is obvious. A kola-nut usually has two equal halves. This halving depicts that the two halves identical or identical twining if this occurs in humans. In human biological terms, the *nuts* shared a genetic maker which was gotten from the same *mother tree* or a branch of the kola-nut tree.

Therefore, any incestuous violation by persons of the same mother, who had shared the same breast milk from their mother requires the "breaking away" of the relationship.

Note here that this, "breaking away process" seems to negate the Biblical marriage declaration and affirmation of the Biblical African Origin): {*whatever, god has put together must be put asunder by man, the Sumoe-nu*}).

In addition, after this purification process any children resulting from the incestuous relationship between the couples must be taken away forever by the **Sumoeh** officers and given to the female's family to be raised as one of their own Damby member. The father of the incestuous birthing will for ever loose his parental rights to the children. This is what is meant by the term cutting away of the kola-nut.

2) WOO-GBASEE

This process may have found its root in the ancient peoples regards for the dog as evidenced in the Bible as briefly explained below.

DOGS AND BIRDS: THE BIBLICA VIEWS

DOG

Dogs like birds feed on carrion, and were considered scavengers especially in the cities, thus the Mosaic Law recommended throwing to the dogs flesh that had been torn by wild beast (Exod. 22:3).

Morally unclean persons are called dogs. God's Law to Israel stated "you must bring the hire of harlot the price of a dog (male prostitute), "likely a *pederast*; one who practice anal intercourse, especially with a boy," into the house of Jehovah your God for any vow, because they are something detestable to Jehovah your God even both of them." (De 23:18). All those who, like scavenger dogs of the streets, practice disgusting things, such as sodomy, lesbianism, viciousness and cruelty, are debarred from access to New Jerusalem (Rev 2:15; Php 3:2).

The enemies of Jehovah's servants were likened to dogs, and so were the Gentiles (Psalm 22:16, 20; 59:6, 14; Matt 15:26, 27. Jesus compared person having no appreciation for spiritual things to dogs saying: "Do not give what is holy to dogs" (Matt 7:6).

The dog's habit of lapping water while at the same time keeping its eyes open to scan the surrounding conditions was referred to when God prescribed a test for the volunteers of Gideon's army. Only those who were alert, lapping up water from their hands, "just as a dog laps" were to be chosen for the fight against Midian, (Judges7).

This process involves the "beaten" of a dog. The couples are depicted as dogs precisely, because, any person capable of an incestuous behavior is like a dog that gets offspring from its own mother, bitches, or dogs etc. Therefore, the habit must be 'beaten' out of the "dogs". In this case, the two dogs are the two couples who are stripped of their clothes; and their naked bodies beaten by the Sumoeh members arranged on the left and right of the couples as they walk between them.

For the fact that the *Sandur* chiefdom is the only chiefdom in the Kono District credited **with Rites of this purification** process is also; an indication of their ancient religious significance in the District.

An example of a family **sun-yu-u** is as follows: **Sangah-cheh** *(financial support from members in time of bereavement), Gbandie-Kondoneneh (financial assistance in time of sickness);* and consistent support are ingredient in the strength of the Sun-gu-u.

However, when this support is lacking in a family, it results in the break down of the family unit.

CHAPTER SEVEN

The Laws of Swoon-Yu-U or Damby

Since it seems the Kono formally have to select their mates from within the same class but outside the clan; then, what kind of family group is the best from which to seek an ideal mate? According to the Ancient Kono tradition, the ideal marriage partner is one's cross cousin; hence, there are numerous cases of cross-cousin marriage, still being practiced among the Mandinkas and other Mande speakers.

In these Mande families that still practice the 'Old-ways'—if a girl's paternal aunt has a boy and the boy's maternal uncle is the father of the girl, then the boy's family has priority in sending a match-maker to negotiate for the girl's hand. For this reason the maternal uncle dare not marry his daughter into another family. Likewise, the son of a female's maternal uncle has the same priority over her, a daughter of his paternal aunt. Therefore, there is a mutual marriage relationship between the sons and daughters of the two families. One can find many evidences of this form of cross-cousin marriages even now from Kono kinship terms. The terms used to establish relationship points to cross-cousin marriages. These terms have being isolated and would be fully explained the Notes. (The terms associated with marriage seem to suggest that the Kono must have had similar marriage customs.

The Mandinkas for instance, when they were not known as a tribe call Kono, they must have practiced cross-cousin marriages. Therefore, it is these form of marriages that we are going to **explore.**

Tain-sa-musu, tain-sa-kai, nii-mor-moe, bia-musu, bia-gai. Dai-moe, and dain-na-musu are some of such terms that indicated very close *blood ties*.

Because of his marriage to maternal uncle's daughter, the boy also calls his father-in-law maternal uncle and his mother-in-law maternal uncle's wife. Hence the son-in-law is also the sister's son. On the other hand, because of her marriage to the son of her paternal aunt's family, the girl calls her husbands mother paternal aunt and her husband's father paternal aunt's husband.

Cross-cousin marriage is not unilateral, but multilateral in terms of relationship. The boy also sometimes marries the daughter of the paternal aunt; so he calls his mother-in-law paternal aunt and his father-in-law paternal aunt's husband. In this case, the son-in-law is also the wife's brother's son. The girl is sometimes married to the son of the maternal uncle; therefore she calls her husband's parents maternal uncle and maternal uncle's wife. In that case the daughter-in-law is the husband's sister's daughter.

Since it seems the Kono have practiced cross-cousin marriage for generations, there are special kinship terms of address between wife's parents (bia-musu for wife's mother and bia-gai, wife's older male relatives including the father. Nii-moe is word used for both younger male and female relatives, and son-in-law (biaa-gai, whether old or young)], and between father-in-law and daughter-in-law [dain-na-musu] are bifurcated from the wife's clan, which in which in turn is bifurcated from the mother's clan. Since the Kono seem to put great value on male gender this may explain the maternal uncles (bain-du-moe-nu are so important in all Kono children's lives. The relationship between the patrilineal and matrilineal clans is the closest as they are continuously interlinked through marriage.

The Konos have turned away from cross marriages; however, their cousins Mandingos retain this custom, as described above.

Because of their priority in marriage, Kono cross-cousins treat each other quite differently from the way brothers and sisters treat each other. Cross-cousins of the opposite sex who have preferential marriage privileges can play and flirt with each other and eventually have sexual relationship after marriage. This is quit different from the strict relationship between brother and sisters, who never act loosely toward each other. Therefore, it can be seen how customs and traditions mold individual behavior and attitudes and how they regulate interpersonal obligations and duties.

Kono preferential marriage is limited to cross-cousins, including one and father's sister's daughter or one's and mother's brother's daughter, mothers sister's daughter and one are also prohibited from contracting marriage relationships. This prohibition of maternal parallel-cousin marriage is quit different from the **Mandika**) custom and may be due to the Kono emphasis on the maternal lineage.

The children of the maternal aunt are treated in the same way as the children of the paternal uncle. In the Kono language, mother's sisters children are also addressed as (**N'dai-su-neh-nu**), denoting a relationship similar to that between brothers and sisters. Therefore they are accorded the same treatment.

To make it easy to understand, one has to make a mental chart to indicate the marriage relationship of the interdiction of a marriage relationship between brothers and sisters of the same generation and between male and female cousins of different categories.

An indication that the Kono must have had some kind of association with the ancient world of the Egyptians, Hebrews and other Biblical Tribes is found in the Hebrew Tradition narrated in the Book of Root. This Tradition is examined against the facts of the Kono Damby Tradition credited to the Jews.

SECTION III

THE LEVIRATE LAW IS FULLY COVERED IN VOLUME 1

THE KONO FARMING CALENDAR OR SCHEDULE AS

SINCE THIS VOLUME IS ABOUT FOOD, I HAVE DECIDED TO ADD A SEPARATE SECTION IN THIS BOOK ON THE KONO FARMING CALENDER OR SCHEDUL AS ILLUSTRATED BELOW.

Furthermore, this section may help you to understand the next chapter discussed from the Book of Ruth.

In addition, the totemic foods/animals picked by the Kono and foods chosen as totemic by the various Damby founders indicate that the ancient Kono were farmers and hunters or agricultural groups.

CHAPTER EIGHT

Kono Farming Calendar

WITH THE MONTHS OF YEAR IN KONO

DECEMBER-JANUARY (Pegbaa-Dondomakone)

The end of January is the appropriate time for those intending to farm the rice grains, the staple food of the Konos to start the gathering process. Besides the work tools, the farmer would need variety of seeds, such as rice, corns, beans pumpkins (squash), cotton, maize, sesame (Benin), millet, etc. By the time the gathering phase is over, he would have also finished harvesting his main farm.

Therefore, after harvesting the main farm, his swamp, (in Kono **Bu-uu**) in December or early January, then he must search for a suitable site for his next farm which may be a **gbagbah** (a small farm land in close approximation to a swamp, which he selects with strict obedience to the ancient laws as well as recognition of sacred sites and signs etc. Once a site for his new farm site is selected; the rituals begin as explained below.

He shows a boundary line, between him and others by brushing patches of grass and trees in a certain geometric shapes, this map may be in a form of a circle, square, triangle or a line, these serve as markers to warn others that this particular area of land had already been chosen as a potential farm site.

If the farmer is a member of the poro or poneh and this is usually the case', his marker would be a sign of the poro called **Mandah,** a split bush pole (*staff of Tao*) with a leaf stuck in the top of the stick. A leaf is a sign of life that tells us that seeds produce tree that produce leaves which dry up, fall and are no more, but the seeds continue to beget new seeds through the process of death and rebirth), like a seed that dies in the soil in order to produce new seeds.

Since farming involves complex decision making he may seek advice from the dead ones if he chooses, he may consult the oracles, a sorcerer, who the Kono call **ya-waa-gba-simoeh, *and also*** commonly knowing as the "looking-gron," in Krio or *ya-waa-gba-simoeh* in the Kono language to determine whether the place he has chosen is not only suitable for farming but to know if he will get a good harvest.

As in all African cultures there are places in the village bushes where farming, gardening and other agricultural activities are forbidden for various reasons.

In some places farms are prohibited due to the possessory rights of spirits—good ones as well as bad ones.

It has already been said that the Kenos believe in reincarnation of the dead even though we may not see them, they do exist. Therefore, some areas of the bushes may be the homes of these resurrected ones, who are found in possession of the bush and must first be consulted in order to get their permission to farm a particular area.

Depending on findings, the **ya-waa-gba-simoeh *or*** sorcerer may prescribe **yaasi** (sacrifice), a peace offering, such as rice flour and kola-nuts; the suspending of a bell from a frame on a cord of white satin may be suggested. In some cases, the farmer may be commanded to make peace offering of fang-**ada-ma**: "whatever you have"—"rice, cassava, banana, bush yams, etc. A place to make the sacrifice will be designated, usually in a valley, near a tree, on the farm path, or near a big stream places of choice. The farmer may also be warned in a dream.

FEBRUARY THROUGH MARCH (Duundu-umba—Nyawai)

FIAMACKOH-SONAH (FIAMAKƆESƆNA).

By this time the farmer must finish the brushing and cutting the necessary trees at the farm site while at the same time looking for certain signs from mother nature that let him know whether he is moving according to schedule or not. The first sign he will look for is rain, called by the Kono *fiamckoh-sonah (fiamakƆεsƆna)*. These words literally mean "the rain which washes the bush." This rain is the showers of blessings that all life was waiting for when the ground is soaked, the termites, which come out three times a year, make their first appearance.

FIACHEH—BII

Farmers call them *fiacheh—bii*, "bush-brushing termites." kƆntεsƆna

While cutting or felling the trees on his farm, he expects a second rain, this the Kono calls *kƆntεsƆna*, and the termites come out for the second time.

KƆntebii-nu

These second sets of termites are now called *kƆntebii-nu*, "tree cutting or felling termites." If the farmer has not reached the stage of work which coincides with the appropriate arrival of the termites, then he has cause to worry for he now knows that he is running behind.

EARLY APRIL(Bu-kuku-u)
Seneh-ma-minda-bii-nu or senemindabiinu

Around this time of the year, the farmer starts looking for other signs such as certain changes in the weather. Since it has already rained once, he knows that it is time to burn the brushings and cut trees.

This burning the farm site must coincide with the third and final coming out of the termites which are now called *Seneh-ma-minda-bii-nu* or **senemindabiinu.** By this time any farmer who has not burned his farm site has cause to be worried: The rains will be falling three times a week now, and his farm may not burn properly.

Note here the three appearances of termites with accompany rains may be equated with certain phases in human pregnancy called **trimesters**

END OF MAY(KOO OR kO-OH)
THE FARMER TAKES THE PLOUGH

After burning his farm site, the farmer now makes the necessary steps to sow the seeds. At the appropriate time he begins the ploughing phase. He does this by first broadcasting the rice seeds at the right spots on farm. The rice seeds may be mixed with other seeds such as corn, okra, small beans, cotton, benne, and cucumber seeds etc,.

JUNE-JULY (SOSOE-NALOE)
Division of labor by gender

At this time **gender roles** relating to the labor on the farm becomes apparent. The wives or women weed out the rice while the men fence the farm to keep out the cutting-grass (cane rat), and other animals that may come to feed on the growing crop and thereby destroying it. Most of these animals get attracted by the smell of the young rice plants.

END OF JULY THROUGH AUGUST(T NALOE—TAAFE)

Kpasa construction As the first signs of grains appear on the rice stems the farmer must now construct a high platform which the Kono calls **Kpasa** to be used for driving birds away from the young rice seeds. The **Kpasa** must be the highest structure on the farm in order to allow the farmer to see from one end of the farm to the other or in short to enable him to see all four corners of the farm.

Mid-August through September (Taafe-Saa)
THE HARVEST.

'first grain offering'

Gbafu

The first soft rice harvested is beaten to make a flat cereal-like flour called **gbafu**. **This gbafu** will serve as **the first grain offering** and is set out for the farm's spirits of the ancestors that reside on the farm.

Senge, kundu-a-sa-sain-neh (or bayai-a—sa-sain-neh)

If there is a **Senge, a place of worship under a huge** tree (associated with ancestral spirits) on the farm, the rice flour will be wrapped in a leaf and put underneath it; otherwise, it will be put under the **kundu-a-sa-saineh** (or **ba-yai-a-sa-sain-neh)**, this is the stone where the farm's machetes are sharpened.

It is believed that this stone contains spirits of the dead ones. Some of the rice flour is scattered on the ground for visiting spirits, the bad ones (spirits) who didn't help the farm are invited to participate in the feast but are reminded to be good and are held to an implied contractual agreement that they will all return to the spirit world at the end of the feast, the forgetfulness of the farmer to dismiss them after the rituals gives them no right to stay after the feast is over.

In the evening, when the farmer returns to his house in the village, he again performs similar rituals as the one done in the day time in the farm. Rice flour is set out or inside at the door of the house (if the ceremony is performed by a man), or near the family's drinking water (if it is performed by a woman).

Beaten rice or rice flour is also offered, and the family calls on their ancestors and deceased parents by name: *"Call the ones I don't know, along with your friends, and come in the morning."* The ancestors are asked to insure the family's good health, to prevent discord, and to protect family members from accidents.

In the morning rice is cooked for them, and after several hours it is eaten by the young children. The basin is provided in which everyone washes hands before and after eating. Some of the water from the basin where the hands were washed is sprinkled in the house as sign of collective act of interceding for the well being of the family. The remaining grains of rice are scattered throughout the house.

BUI-KOR-TEMOEH-NU (Harvest Magicians)

After the feast of the 'first grain offering; and other' sacred ceremonies and rituals, the harvesting may start. If the portion of the farm that is ready to be harvested is very large, the farmer may decide to call in the 'harvest Magicians who the Kono call **BUI-KOR-TEh-MOEH-NU** meaning *medicine harvester*. This author was privileged to witness these men in action when they were invited by her father Year to harvest the family farm.

Also see book of Ruth in the Holy Bible for the Kono link to "harvesters".

BAYAH IN GBAIN-DAI-YAH (Rice Barn in swamp-farm)

The harvested rice is stored temporarily, either in the rice barn, or in a *kɔgbin-neh*—a *"pile of rice."* The rice is measured as follows:

> 3 b*ofadɔndɔ* (3 handfuls) make one **kandadɔndɔ *(1 tie of rice stalk).***
> 3 *kandadɔndɔ* make one *kɔchidɔndɔ* (bundle of rice stalk). (One such tie makes one or more **tropence** pans of rice.)
> 10 *kɔchidɔndɔ* make one *sɔɔdɔndɔ*, or *kɔchitanɛ*, which equals 30 or more pans of beaten rice.
> When relatives come for rice, it is customary to give them **kandafea** (two-thirds of a tie), or *kɔchidɔndɔ*; rarely will they leave with *sɔɔdɔndɔ.*

The rice is stored by **Sɔɔdɔndɔ** *(Sow-don-doh);* a small farm may produce thirty or fifty of these, a large farm may produce up to 100 or more depending on size and type of the harvest result. After the rice has been bundled and counted, it is locked into the rice barn. The key is held by the First or the trusted favorite (senior) wife so that she can take out the rice as needed. If the man does not trust her, he can keep the key himself, and ration the rice out to her as she needs for family use.

Therefore, for the Kono, Seeds like words of faith are already in the Historical Womb of Mother Nature waiting, (**Konu**-*to wait)* the proper water, (ba-yee), to water them into growth and harvest time.

Thus, the seed has to be properly watered in order to have a proper harvest, (Luke 17:3-6),

Heart, seed, words, soul, or grain are one and the same thing. When we change our words, we change our hearts and words in order to harvest good seeds, and thus, to uplift our souls, our hopes must be of faith.

NOW!

The KONO and **THE LEVIRATE LAW** in the Kono culture, one also has rights to farmland by virtue of membership in a patrilineage. Women may also obtain farmland through patrilineal affiliations, although this is unusual and will be discussed further in Chapter. While the paramount chief legally owns the land in his chiefdom, lineage elders hold historically validated de facto rights to tracts of farmland.

Kono lineages act as corporate groups to disperse land to their male members. Although ideologically, all male lineage members are entitled to land that was cultivated by their ancestors, contemporary elders decide what land will be farmed and who is entitled to work the best land. Lineages may also, at their discretion, disperse land to non lineage members who have attached themselves as clients to particular elders in exchange for services for a percentage of the crop.

Lineage elders who are descendants of the **Gbenseneh,** *Sandunu,* and *Mongoeh,* clans control access to farmland in the area around **KainKordu, Gbenseh.** (Other clans predominate in other sections of the chiefdom, or in other Kono chiefdoms.)

Ties to the clan founders and the relative status of sub lineages are ritually validated in pilgrimages to *Kongo-kor-tina*, mountain giving place or thanks giving to a mountain place or in some villages, *Senge Kor*. There, the narrator-**(Senge-ya-sor)** would recite the lineage elders from the most recent dead to as far back in time as he can. Some *Senge-ya-sor* claims they can recite the history of the lineage to it ancient founders.

In contrast, matrilineal ties are used to evaluate the identity resources available in ancient and contemporary time and to judge which affiliations are most likely to bring the best results for the individual *(See the genealogy of Jesus in the Book of Luke).*

Thus, matrilineal ties while less apparent than patrilineal ties, are an equally important facet of identity. While affiliation is always complementary, it is custom that prescribes while social structure decrees "the form this complementary affiliation will take in a given society")

The Kono practice the levirate, which means that a man marries the widow of his deceased patrilineal male relative whether an elder or younger male relative. As a whole, the Kono levirate tends to keep the womenfolk within the clan. Once a woman has entered a clan, she is not supposed to remarry into another, but can only be transferred by marriage within the clan so that she will remain forever its member. At least this must have been the intention of the Ancient.

THE LEVIRATE LAW OF MARRIAGE IS ALSO KNOWN AS MARRIAGE TRANSFERENCE

The levirate is known as "marriage transference within the clan branch". Transferring the marriage to an elder or younger brother of the deceased's generation is considered good form. If there is no blood brother, then a male paternal cousin from the nearest in kinship to the most distant is also acceptable. The practice of marriage transference has had a long history and prevails among the Kono everywhere. Today the levirate is practiced not only within the same generation, but there is also the practice of the nephew's marrying the widow of father's younger brother or the younger uncle's marrying the widow of brother's son.

Marriage transference of a widow is limited mainly to the clan kin of her deceased husband's generation or to his father's younger brother, his brother's son and others.

The Kono population must have been very small that the tradition of marriage transference within the clan branch may also serve the function of solving the population and sex problem. From the standpoint of demography, a woman's remarriage increases the chances for her to have children and clan progeny. From the standpoint of sex, a woman can continue to remarry within the clan after her husband's death-no matter how many husbands she has had-while a man can take a young girl outside the clan or a widow of his own clan for a second wife after the death of the first. For this reason, the Kono whether male of female, can heave sexual fulfillment in life an there are no widows or widowers in the Kono society.

MONOGAMY VS. POLYGAMY

Monogamy must have been the general marriage pattern of the Kono occasionally, but very seldom, they practice polygamy, especially in full obedience to the Levirate Laws. There are enough evidence to suggest they seldom practiced polygamy which moreover must have been also limited to Kono chiefs and wealthy families. Polygamy must have been prohibited in society; but because of their loose sexual concept,(levirate laws) polyandry is sometimes secretly practiced.

Polygamy is often motivated by the political ambition of Kono leaders who want to expand their influence through the connections of their wives families. In a Kono polygamous family, wives have equal social status. They call each other sisters. Without regard to their own ages, the first wife is the elder sister and the second wife the younger sister. Each wife has a separate household and property, but in some family wives and concubine stay together but have unequal social position. Before the Kono man takes a second wife, he has to appease his first wife by offering her gifts. He also has to reach in former days an understanding with his wife's brothers by entertaining them with food and wine. Without their consent in advance, he may run into trouble and have disputes that will develop into a clan feud.

As a whole, these marriages practices not only regulate the Kono sexual life and their kinship and clan structure, but also their daily behavior and even their political and economic activities. The marriage relationship has the same importance in Kono society as in other societies. Marriage is one of the biggest event and one of the most important transitional stage in life as a young man and woman go from love to marriage and from marriage to the establishment of the family.

FAMILY LOVE OR LAW OF THE COVENANT:
THE ISSUE OF PRIMONITUR

The early Israelites like the ancient Konos had a strong sense of family, as is true of most tribal societies. It was the family, rather than the individual, that counted. Possessions belonged to the family as a whole, and no person was truly dead if he left sons behind who could inherit the possessions and hold the ancestral name in reverence. This was one of the reasons why it was so distressing for a man to die without sons. It was a much more real death that way.

The Law guarded against this and said:

In this way, the widow kept her position as a legal wife; she was no concubine or handmaiden. What's more, her son could then inherit her first husband's property. It was a kind of legal continuation of the first marriage, giving the widow security and the dead husband remembrance.

This custom was called "Levirate marriage" from the Latin word levir meaning "husband's brother."

CHAPTER NINE

A Famous Example of the Levirate Law from the Holy Bible is Found in the Book of Ruth.

INTRODUCTION

The best-known and earliest example of this custom involved Judah himself. He was the fourth son of Jacob and the man who was considered to be the ancestor of the people of Bethlehem and all the other towns of the tribe of Judah.

Judah had three sons: Er, (Aiah), Onan (Aunah), and Shelah (Soleh) are common Kono names; and the Bible says:

Judah found a wife for his eldest son, Er (Kono-Aiah); her name was Tamar. But Judah's eldest son Er (Aiah) was wicked in the Lord's sight, and the Lord took his life. Then Judah told Onan (Kono-Aunnah) to sleep with his brother's wife, to do his duty as the husband's brother and rise up issue for his brother. (Genesis 38:6-8)

Onan *(Kono-Aunnah)*, however, refused to do his dead brother this service and he died too. Judah was reluctant, then, to marry Tamar to his third son, Shelah, feeling that the woman was "bad luck" and that his third son might die too.

Tamar, remaining a widow and resenting this lowly estate, used trickery to force Judah himself to give her children. At first, Judah was in a rage, but then he said:

"She is more in the right than I am, because I did not giver her to my son, Shelah (Soleh)."

(Genesis 38:26)

This old legend about Judah points out how this respected ancestor valued the institution of the Levirate marriage. It also shows how Onan was punished by God for refusing his part in it.

The Bible also points out how well this particular incident turned out, for Tamar who had twin sons, of which Judah was the father. These were named Perez and Zerah, and they were the ancestors of the most important clans among the descendants of Judah. SEE BOOK OF RUTH

CHAPTER TEN

The Levirate Law and the African Idea of a Family

CYCLES OF POWER: ANIMAL TANAH (TOTEMIC PROHIBITION)

INTRODUCTION

The Kono have animals to which they relate as their Tana or Totemic Prohibition. Some of these animals are listed below.

To fully understand the implications of the Solleh family Genesis which continue below as an example of the importance of: bloodline issues", in the Kono community certain key terms needs to be introduced and explained.

MOGENITOR: is a Kono-or Mande word with several meanings. However to get these clear meanings, one must break the Kono word into its component parts, i.e., **Moe**, + **gena**, + **tor**, These words yield the following meanings, Mo**genator, this word interprets to mean** a 'spirited person' or a person is a spirit.

Moe is a Kono word meaning *'person'*, **geina** is a Kono or Mande (the cousins of the Kono people); the word means, *'Spirit'*; and **tor or toeh**, the essence of a person means, *'name'*. Therefore, the word **mogenito**r means 'a person, is a 'spirited being' or 'a person has a name of a spirit'. Hence, this confirms . . . *"let us make man in our image and likeness".*

DAMBY PRIMOGENITORS

Pen-pehn, is a Kono word meaning, "before the beginning of what was handed to us humans from which we came to know the meaning of the words *Pen-pehn* "the Beginning of the beginning".

Let me break in down:

Pehn in the Kono language means any of the following words: *first, before, or 'to start with . . . '.* Pehn-pehn on the other hand is a Kono word meaning "First and foremost", 'before the beginning of 'times, we now know as the "beginning". In short, the word *"Pehn-pehn'* parallels the English or Latin word "Pri", while the word "Pre" is paralleled with the Kono word *"Pehn"*.

Now, since the English word '**pri'**, means "before the beginning of the 'beginning'," and the Kono word '**pehn-pen' has** a parallel in meanings with the word "Pri" such as 'before' the beginning of the beginning". I therefore, maintain that, both the Kono and the English words have a common etymology or origin.

Clearly then, the word **pri·mo·gen·i·tors** from the Kono perspective would mean, 'in the beginning before the beginning or 'in pre-historic times', *before a person became spirited being and become known as the original ancestor . . .* 'This would mean that in the beginning of 'prehistoric times', persons were not 'spirited' nor did they have names nor did what we now know as the word "people", tribe" . . . were not identified as such or did not exist.

The logical conclusion or implications here is that man developed ideas and founded belief system, religions and cities after *he acquired a name of a spirit.* This conclusion is exactly what the ancient Kono words are telling us. Therefore, the understanding of various Kono words would eventually lead to **solving the riddle of the Sphinx**.

Furthermore, the implications of theses claims lead us yet to another conclusion that the Kono Damby founders were all males. However, this posit a question; *how did the Pig which the Kono call Koiehnyah get in the Kono Damby pectoral Tradition to become depicted as prohibited Damby Animal to Kono females or Pengusanu?*

Moreover, this posit yet another question; *how did the Pig which the Kono call Koiehnyah get in the Kono Damby pectoral Tradition to become depicted as prohibited Damby Animal to Kono females or Pengusanu?*

As already stated above, the Kono Damby **pri·mo·gen·i·tors** were the first 'pre-historic' "humans" who became the ancestors and founders of the Kono Damby Families.

Furthermore, since the first Damby groups were twelve in numbers, this also affirms that these first Kono Damby founder though may not have been by this name had Astrological as well as Astronomical knowledge from their original home. Judging from the Kono names, one can put up a good argument that they may have either came from the Sirius System or had a very close contact with ancient Atlantis or Egypt.

In addition, these primogenitors also, chose not only certain animals, but plant and vegetables as well to represent each of the Damby's original male primogenitors for as long as the progeny of each primogenitor exists on the earth realm. Since there were originally twelve Damby animals including plant and vegetables, to represent the *bloodlines of the primogenitors, then Bloodlines Issues (Children) is posited in the form of Genetics, DNA and so on.*

Therefore, it is logical here to assume that there were twelve founding primogenitors that chose not only animal totems, but plants, roots and other vegetables were added to those choices made.

Since the Kono male primogenitor included all future Kono male children in the Damby conceptual prohibitions, they thus, had decided the fate of all future generations as well, on that day the choice of Damby Tradition was established. Therefore, we must assume here, that the fates of not only the male children but also female children were also carefully examined. However, most of these records are lost in the 'burning sands of 'Time'; thus making the determination of the legal issues attached to the Damby Tradition run into legal problems. This being the problem, then, the term Primogeniture, as explained below, runs into problems too.

CHAPTER ELEVEN

Damby Primogeniture

INTRODUCTION

Furthermore, since the Damby Tradition, right or wrong seems to be founded on the <u>supremacy of males</u> over females, then, the term *Primogeniture* must be examined for its validity.

The term *primogeniture,* in the English language is a term used to establish the state of been the 'first-born child' of a set of parents in a family.

It is also used to determine *'the right of the first-born child', usually the eldest son, of the father to inherit the parents' entire estate, it is also called the first-born's right of inheritance.*

In ancient Damby times, this right may usually have belonged to the first-born son of the father in a polygamous home, where there is more than one wife. The rights of the first-born son will be discussed below; but would be fully covered in volume III of this Damby series.

THE MAJOR PROBLEM FACING THE CONCEPT OF PRIMOGENITURE

However, the problem presented by the Concept of Primogeniture is this; the Damby does not seem to address the issue of what happens if the father's first born son dies; nor did it address the issues of twinning where one or mor of the twin sets die. The Damby Tradition failed to address the position of the surviving sons or daughters according to the order of their birth to their respective mothers and to the father especially in a **polygamous** home; and according to the Naming Tradition of the Kono.

Furthermore, in the Kono Tradition as already explained above, children are named based on the order of the mother's pregnancy; and this fact does not change even if the child was born a premature and died. If it is determined that it was a baby, the child's positional name cannot be given to another or abandoned if the child dies. Therefore, based on this criteria, a second son of the father from the same mother or an other cannot assert the *argument of Primogeniture* for the purpose of securing for himself the right of the first-born child, because these are usually reserved for the eldest son, of the father who stands to inherit the parents' entire estate. Hence, as the term indicates, it *is also called the first-born's right of inheritance*

Furthermore, as pointed out above, the words "Pri" and "Penhn-pehn" have a common etymology as explained above. Therefore, the word "Primogeniture" would interpret to mean "before the first son or child become known or named as the first child

WHAT THEN IS IN THE NAME OF A KONO CHILD?

In the Kono culture, because the *Naming Tradition starts in the mother's womb*, the head of the Naming Tradition therefore, is the mother and not the father as is the case in the Damby Tradition where the father is a priority. However, there are about six to nine essential facts that must be understood about the Kono Naming Tradition; and they are as follows:

(1) A name is a sound with tonal and rhythmic significance.

(2) A name is a sign—a means by which an individual, animal or a thing is identified or called. It distinguishes one person, animal or things from another.

(3) A name is a symbol. It links a person with a culture, a tradition, and a *family heritage*.

(4) A name represents a person to a community. Through a name, a person takes part in a community in order to fulfill his or her highest purpose for been burn in such community to which

he or she identified with; there by establishing his or her 'cosmic assignment'.

(**5**) A name becomes a symbol of the Kono past. The history of a people is reflected in the names it uses; e.g., the Kono name "*Tanmba*", implies that the ancient people of the tribe had knowledge of not only Egyptian cosmology but also the so-called *Kabbalah*, an acclaimed Jewish mysticism based on Sephirothic system of *ten divine names*. These three systems, the Kono, Egyptian and Jewish mysteries schools use the number ten as their starting point.

(**6**) A name is a number. It identifies the position of an individual in the birth order according to the mother's pregnancy; e.g., Sia (1), Kumba (2), etc.

Therefore, in order to understand the Kono birth order or positional and gender-based Naming Tradition from the point of view of the Kono, a basic understanding of the numerology of the ancient Kono people is essential. That is, to determine which name belongs to the birth order and the gender of a person, the ancient Kono developed a standardized logic structure to compare the two genders. *See Kono Gold or Koine Gold: By Kumba Femusu Solleh.*

The concept of the primogeniture and its legal implications are fully examined in Volume III. The decision for this move is based on the facts that before any understanding of the Kono Tradition becomes a concerned thoroughly understanding of the source of the Kono belief System is necessary. Alternatively I believe, this understanding can never be established without knowing some facts about the ancient Egyptians and ancient Jewish, people, who received most of the believe systems form the ancients Sources; who in turn, were the remainders of the ancient prehistoric people of ancient Atlantis., the ancestors of the Kono people. Thus, we continue with ancient Egyptians whose records can testify to the claims made in this book below.

As explained in Volume III, in the Solleh family, the father revoked the ancient Hebrew tradition to settle the issue of establishing his primogeniture, which can only be understood in the light of the gnosis, (Kono Nor-hoh-sonn, meaning 'I know') of the ancient terms, Damby Primogenitors and Damby Primogeniture already explained above. As you read the Solleh saga, you will realize that the Kono Damby Tradition revolves around these two bloodline words. In addition, the father, by revoking what came down to us as ancient Hebrew Law clearly shows that the ancient Kono and the ancient Hebrew acquired their knowledge from a common source, the ancient Egyptians.

DAMBY *PRIMOGENITORS AND DAMBY PRIMOGENITURE: THE LEGAL ISSUES*

*To re-emphasize what h*as already be stated above, the phrase Kono Damby **pri·mo·gen·i·tors,** refers to those individuals in the Kono village or family groups who were <u>not only</u> the first male ancestors but were the founders of the Kono Damby Families.

The term **primogeniture** is a term used to establish the state of been established as the first-born male or the first-born child of a set of parents in a Damby family.

This author was born in a set of twins, a male and female set. This author's twin was not *only a male child but was also the first-born male child to my mother, the first or the Damby wife and my father.*

However, my twin brother died just after birth leaving my father with no male son to fill the position of the office of *first-born male child*.

Nonetheless, according to the Kono Naming Tradition, no other male child born of any wife can now fill his position as the first male, and twin brother. He was born not only as first male twin called *Sahr Fengai*; but was also *the first-born son from the dead* based on the Kono cosmology. Therefore, he was born with all the rights of primogeniture

Therefore, if justice is to be served and validated, both the Naming and the Damby Traditions must be put to the test in order to pass the test of their true original definitions.

According to the Kono Tradition, my twin brother must maintain not only his <u>positional name</u> but also, his <u>rightful title, as the Solleh rightful primogeniture.</u>

On the other hand, according to the same Kono Naming Tradition and Belief System relating to twinning, and other multiple births, the tradition stated that when a set of twins or other multiple birth are born and one or more of the children die, the Kono belief is that the surviving twin as absorbed the powers of the dead twin. This implies, that all the rights of the dead twin has been past on to the surviving twin.

This been so, we must now put this belief system of the Kono Naming Tradition to the test of time.

Since a name is power, then it must go without much a do, and say that the surviving twin not only has absorbed the spiritual powers but has also, *absorbed the rights to the powers of the position of the deceased twin*. This means then, that even though the surviving twin can <u>not</u> according to Kono Tradition take the position of the surviving twin, in this case, the position of <u>primogeniture, due to the surviving twin's female gender position,</u> the surviving twin has earned the right to hold or occupy that position in the name of her deceased twin brother.

Furthermore, the Kono Damby practice what the ancient Hebrews call *the Levirate Law which parallels the Kono* Damby Tradition, therefore, there must have been a **Law of Primogeniture** for surviving twin for the purpose of *the first-born's right of inheritance. Furthermore, the Damby Laws included females in the Levirate Law for the purpose of marriage transference under which this author has acquired her father's wives and property.*

Now the issue posited in the Solleh family is this, as a female of the surviving male twin <u>primogeniture, has this author also acquired the rights of the primogeniture" as well?</u>

The answer clearly, is yes!

See Volume III for more on this issue.

PART II

INTRODUCTION

The Kono Damby Tradition and the Sign of Aquarius

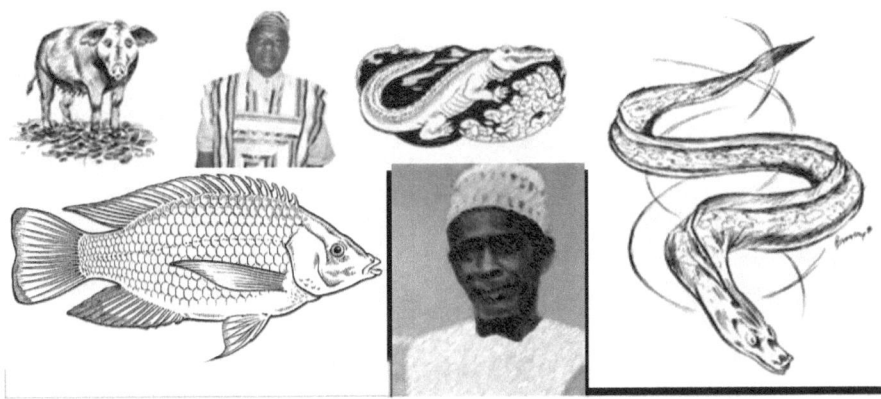

The leadership in the Kono District is pointing to self fulfilling prophecy for the age of the water peoples: ***fish, crocodile, snakes or serpents, otters and pigs*** as explained below.

After much reflection, I have come to the conclusion that I must start this section on the Damby tradition with the Aquarius people including the parts played by the Damby Animals in the Kono Traditon specially parts played by the *Pengusah* Damby for obvious reasons. One of such reasons is pin-pointing the origin and direction of the Kono present leadership trend in the Government of Sierra Leone as a whole. Thus, I start this section with the Pengusah Damby who because of the crocodile, their totemic animal (*Fayeetana-ti-nu*) at least for male is a fitting representative for the water people. Jesus , whose sign is the fish also represent this Damby group including the Yam Damby (*Gbenseneh-nu*),

The Vice President of Sierra Leone to start with, is from the Pengusah Damby and that is sufficient enough reason to realize that Pengusah Damby is in the seat of the Kono Political Throne of Power.

In addition, among most of the Kono chiefs particularly the Gbenseh chiefs, majority claim a Patrilineal background from the Sandur chiefdom, the home of the *Pengusah Damby*.

CHAPTER ONE

The Fish Totemic Damby

N'YEH-TANATINU OR SANN-TANA-TI-NU: ARE COLLECTIVELY CALLED

Nyenanu and their totemic animals are the lizards, Iguana, **FISH and all reptile family**

There were certain fishes that were not eaten by Egyptians, because according to the Ancient narrative, Typhon or Set, the Egyptian god had killed and divided the body of the God—Osiris into 14 parts and threw one part into the River Nile, where per Plutarch it was eaten by three fishes. Thus, there are three types of fish that are not eaten by the Egyptians.

The Kono word for fish is N'YEN: a cold-blooded water vertebrate-gilled animal that lives in water. It typically has jaws, fins, scales, a slender body, a two-chambered heart, and gills for providing oxygen to the blood.

Fish are amazing creatures. Some are bright and colorful such as rainbow fish, others are plain. They are excellent swimmers and their life in water is symbolical of the primordial fluid of the womb, motherhood and woman.

Those with this totem should be dynamic and constantly in transition. If a fish enters your dreams, its time for movement and change.

The subconscious and unconscious mind has always been associated with water. Fish are linked with the elements of the unknown and hold the energy of transformation.

SANEH is the Kono word for <u>eel</u>, a fish with a long thin body resembling that of a snake, smooth skin without scales, and reduced fins. Freshwater eels are typically known to migrate to the ocean to spawn. *San-tana-tinu* is the Kono name for a group of Kono family group whose totemic prohibition is a fish call eel with the Kono name. Saneh. The Kono word Saneh, interprets to mean 'Sa is here'; the Sa in the instance refers to the Germ cell or the substance in the sperm.

SEE IMAGES OF CHIEF P.C SAHR FENGAI KAIMACHAINDAIH PLUS OTHER CHEIFS FROM SANDUR, HERE CALLED THE SANDUR CONNECTION

CHAPTER TWO

Who are the Pengusah Totemic Groups?

THE PENGUSA-NU

Sir Milton Margai, the first Prime Minister of independent Sierra Leone, and Dr W. M. Fitzjohn arriving at Marlborough House, London, for the opening of the 1962 Commonwealth Prime Ministers Meeting. Crocodile God (Image #) P.C. KORGBANDAIH

KAMACHIANDAIH II, P.C. SAHR FENGAI KAIMACHIANDAIH III (RIGHT) AND P.C. TAMBA FENGAI ALPHA MANI

IT IS THIS AUTHORS VIEWS THAT OF ALL THE DAMBY GROUPS, THE PENGUSA DAMBY ARE THE CLOSEST TO THE ANCIENT EGYPTIANS IN ORIGIN. BY THIS I MEAN, THE GROUP STILL MENTAINS THE ANCIENT EGYPTIAN MYSTERY TRADITIONS

The Pengusanu, are of two groups, male and female, gender based food prohibitions have been fully discussed in chapters three and four of section one above. They are collectively called **PENGUSA-NU.**

WHO ARE THE PENGUSAH TOTEMIC GROUPS?

Originally, the Pengusah groups were predominantly found in the Sandur chiefdom. However, through the years, their influence spread all over West Africa as explained below.

Pegusahnu are found in the following areas: *Gbaneh, N'gandor*, in places like *Gandorhun*, **Soa** Chiefdom at *Kainkordu* and are represented by the **Gbaindah** and **Foryoh** families. In addition, the Pengusah are found in *Fiamah* Chiefdom; and are found in *Kamara or Kamaah* Chiefdom and represented by **Bor-wu** of *Sukudu*. They are also found in *Nimiyamah* Chiefdom and are represented by the *Toh-o-oh* toh or Torto family. In *Nimikoro* or *Nimiko-oh*, they are represented by the *Mbayoh* family.

The most important thing to note here is that the Pengusah forms the political or ruling classes of warrior Damby families and continue to rule in Kono chiefdoms even today.

BA-MBA-A KONO WORD FOR ALLIGATOR
(ALIGATOR TOTEM FOR MALES ONLY)
Therefore, it may be argued that the Kono people are actually the issues of ancient Egyptians.

Within the totemic system of the Damby, tradition there is a group of people called **Fayee-Tana-tinu. '[Fai i ta Na ti nu]** commonly known as the Pengusanu.** The Fayeetanatinnu is a gender based totemic system. This gender-based system consists of both males and females. Within the Fayeetanatinnu, the males are called 'Bambah'. The Fayeetanatinnu females are called 'pengusanu'.

In all of the Damby totemic systems, there is a prohibition against the eating of certain animals. Because the alligator, the crocodile, lizards, and iguana are taboo or prohibited to the 'Bambah' group these animals are not eaten. This taboo does not apply to the female of the Fayeetanatinnu group.

In the Kono language, the word for Alligator is 'Bambah'. This is why the word for alligator 'Bambah' is also the word for the name of the male totemic group.

Among the Kono people and of all the Chiefdoms only the Sandur Chiefdom is named after the name of a totemic animal of females; and this is the reason why I am paying *some what* full attention to the Pengusah females. However, may be due to some ***mis-haps*** in 'his-story' only males can be come chiefs in a chiefdom named after the totemic animals of females; the Chiefdom is not named after the male totemic animal. Instead, in an attempt to decrease the feminine power, the ancient Elders may have blundered; and as in the Kono Naming Tradition, the Chiefdom is named after the female totemic group. In this case, the name is 'Pengusah', i.e., female Fayeetanatinnu group.

This chief, see image above is the personification of the Great Male *Sayings of the wise* that was reported in the Holy Bible as spoken by Jesus.

That is, the chief's name, the District he represents, (Pengusah) and his attire, reveals much more than meets the eye. The 'initiatory' declaration or 'initiatory' saying *"ALL POWER HAS BEEN GIVEN TO ME BY 'MY FATHER'* is revealed as being very close to the saying of the ancient Egyptians; "My heart, of my mother, my heart of transformations" "I am the rudder of the possessor of the two divine faces wherein his beams are seen." (See Budge Egyptian Book of the Dead (1967:439).

This suggests that the source of the 'initiatory' saying of the ancient Serpents of Wisdom of the Kono Branch and the Egyptians is one and the same.

Therefore, it may be argued that the Kono people are actually the issues of ancient Egyptians.

The Word Ba-Mba Interprets to Mean Mother is my Companion

BA is an ancient word for Mother and M'ba means companion used among women initiates of the same year of initiation: so Ba + M'ba mean Mother's Companion; and who then is the companion of the alligator?

The alligator is called *Fa-Yee*, meaning Father Water or Father of the Waters.

Thus, if the crocodile is called Fa-Yee, which in the Kono language means 'Father Water' and the Alligator, the companion of the crocodile is called Ba M'ba, then, another meaning of Ba M'ba is Mother Water. Therefore, the Bambah must have been the totemic animal for females of the gender-based group called the Pengusah Damby. However, for some odd warp in the history of the Kono, yet to be discovered, the ancient decided to replace the Bambah with the Pig. Thus, the totemic prohibition for the females of the Pengusah Damby is Pig. Thus, in a way one can refer to this Damby group of the Pengusah: the Crocodile (Fayee) and the Alligator (Bambah) Damby being gender based. While, the males are called Bamba the females are called Pengusa. Yet, together (to-get-her), both groups are referred to as Pengusanu.

Why did the ancient Kono substitute the tamer and the smaller crocodile called alligator, which the Kono call Bambah with the Pig? To answer this question we must examine the ancient Egyptian religion or worship of Sobek discussed below.

The male Damby of the crocodile clan or Bamba clan do not eat the alligator or crocodile, but the female Damby of the crocodile clan called Pengusa-nu do not eat the pig, swine boar or hog. But can eat the crocodile or alligator, Iguana and lizards but the males are prohibited from eating them

The word alligator refers to a large reptile that lives near rivers or water, has thick scaly skin, powerful jaws, a long tail, and a shorter and broader snout than a crocodile. Native to: Africa

Leather made from alligator skin is forbidden to alligator clans or Damby.

IGUANA

The Kono word for iguana is kana, which is of the lizard family and a totemic animal to the crocodile Damby, males only. The people or group prohibited from eating or whose totemic animal is the iguana are called 'Kanatanatinu'.

Kana is a large plant-eating lizard with a serrated fringe or crest running along its back from head to tail. Native to: tropical Africa, South and Central America.

LIZARDS (*DAI_YA_AH*): a Kono word for

Lizards are symbols of Mercury due to their rapid motion. Mercury was known as the Messenger of the Gods, whose winged feet traveled infinite distances instantaneously.

CHAPTER THREE

Pengusa-Nu: Animals in Ancient Egypt

The Pengusah are of two groups based on gender differentiations, males and females, collectively called:

PENGUSA-NU

1) BAMBAH GROUP *(MALES ONLY)*: ARE ALSO CALLED *FAH-YEE-TANATI-NU. THE TOTENIC ANIMALS ARE: THE CROCODILE, ALLIGATOR, LIZARD AND IGUANA.*

2) *PENGUSA-NU:*
*(FEMALES ONLY)ARE ALSO CALLED **KHOI-NYAH-TANATINU.** THE TOTEMIC ANIMALS ARE, PIG, SWANE, HUG OR BOAR.*

PIG, *SOW, SWINE, HOG, BOAR*
Greek word—**Khoi'ros**
*Kono word—**Khoi-nyah or Bessie,*** Ancient Kono Su-ukhu
Hebrew—**Chazir**
Latin-**Sus** Domestica
Ancient Egyptian—**sus scrofa**

The pig was an animal sacred to set of ancient Egypt, also known as the god of chaos. According to the ancient Egyptian legend, Set took the form of a black pig and blinded Horus, his brother or uncle then disappeared. Eventually Horus regained his sight. *The eyes of Horus were thought to represent the sun and the moon,* and *the legend of the blinding of the god was a metaphorical explanation of solar and lunar eclipses.* Plutarch says that, once a year, pigs were sacrificed to the moon. This means the lunar worship is link to Damby through the totemic Tradition.

The local breed of domestic pig in ancient Egypt descended from an indigenous ancestor, **sus scrofa**, the Wild Boar.

This animal in the ancient times was numerous and covered a great territory ranging from the Nile Valley, in the Delta, *to the Faiyum area were it was reverend together with the crocodile.*

The Pig was a delicacy to the ancient Greeks-but was taboo by the Mosaic Law *Lev 11:7; Deut 14:8.Thus, it is safe to infer that Moses and his people were of a Pengusa Damby.*

While the Mosaic Law *Lev 11:7; Deut 14:8.* Per Jehovah's ban on eating pork was not necessarily based on health considerations, there were and still are health hazards connected with the use of this animal's meat for food. Since pigs are indiscriminate in their feeding habits, even eating **carrion and offal**, they tend to be infested with various parasitic organisms, including those responsible for diseases such as **trichinosis and ascariasis**.

GLOSSARY WORDS

OFFAL:1. Edible internal organs: the edible, mainly internal organs of an animal, e.g. the heart, liver, brains, and tongue, sometimes regarded as unpalatable. 2. Something thrown away: something discarded as refuse.

CARRION: rotting animal flesh: the rotting flesh of a dead animal.

TRICHINOSIS: disease caused by parasitic worm: a disease caused by infestation with trichinae and marked by fever, muscle pain, and diarrhea, often resulting from eating undercooked pork infected with the larvae

ASCARIASIS: parasitic nematode worm: a parasitic nematode worm, e.g. a common roundworm

The Israelites viewed the swine as loathsome. Hence the ultimate words: "The one offering up a gift—the blood of a pig!" *(Is 66:3).* To the Israelites, few things could have been more inappropriate than a pig with gold-ring in the nose or ring in its snout. And it is to this that *Proverbs 11:22* compared an outwardly beautiful woman who is not sensible.

Although apostate Israelites ate pork (*Is 65:4; 66:17*), the Apocryphal books of First Maccabees *(1:65,)* and Second Maccabees (*6:18, 19; 7: 1,2,*) show that during the foreign domination of Palestine by the Syrian king Antiochus IV Epiphanies with his vicious campaign to stamp out the worship of Jehovah, there were many Jews who refused to eat the flesh of swine, preferring to die for violating the decree of the king rather than to violate the law of God.

It is clear that by the time of Jesus' earthly mission; and due to Hellenistic influence that viewed pork meat as a delicacy, there were apparently quite a number of pigs in Palestine, particularly in the Decapolis region. There was at least one herd of about 2,000 pigs in the country of the Gadarenes. When Jesus permitted the expelled demons that he had expelled to enter this large herd, every last one of the animals rushed over a precipice and drowned in the sea. _ *Matt 8:28-32; Mark 5:11-13.*

ILLUSTRATIVE USE

The inability of swine to recognize the value of pearls was employed by Jesus in illustrating the lack of wisdom in sharing spiritual things with those having no appreciation whatever of spiritual thoughts and teachings. *(Matt 7:6)*. And again in Jesus' illustration of the prodigal son, the degradation to which a young man had sunk was accentuated by his having to hire himself out as a swineherd, and by his willingness even to eat the food of these animals pointed to his fallen state; swineherd was the most despicable occupation for a Jew at the time _ *Luke 15:15,16.*

The apostle Peter compared Christians who revert to their former course of life to a sow that returns to its wallow after having been washed. *(2Pet 2:22)*

However, it is evident that, as relates to the pig, this illustration is not intended to apply beyond the surface appearance of things.

Actually, the pig, under natural conditions, is no dirtier than other animals, although it indulges in wallowing in the mud from time to time in order to cool off in the heat of the summer and to remove external parasites from its hide.

As matter of fact, the pig's indulgence in excessive wallowing in mud can be compared to what the Christians are fund of saying . . . "covered by the blood of Jesus". In esoteric teachings muddy water is emblematic of the coagulated

Menstrual blood that results into a baby and also covers a new born baby.

CHAPTER FOUR

The Crocodile, Alligator, Lizard, Iguana and Swine Totemic Families

IT IS THIS AUTHORS VIEWS THAT OF ALL THE DAMBY GROUPS, THE PENGUSA DAMBY ARE THE CLOSEST TO THE ANCIENT EGYPTIANS IN ORIGIN. BY THIS I MEAN, THE GROUP STILL MENTAINS THE ANCIENT EGYPTIAN MYSTERY TRADITIONS

The Pengusanu, are of two groups, male and female in gender based food prohibitions. This aspect of the Damby Tradition has been fully discussed in chapters three and four of section one above and also, in Section VI below.

These two are collectively called PENGUSA-NU. Therefore, the Pengusanu will not be covered here.

THE IMPORTANCE OF ANIMALS IN ANCIENT EGYPT AND KONO ANUBIS

The Egyptian god Anubis was a jackal-headed man bearing a **was—scepter**, signifying power and authority. In the Kono Tradition, the man who carries the Was-scepter in a form of the 'Toffah' plant is called the **Wuusah;** he acts as the messenger of the Poroh secret society. Therefore, one sure way of knowing that he is on a mission is when he places the toffah across his chest secured by one hand. The toffah plant is his sign of power.

SOBEK (SEBEK, SUCHOS), the crocodile-god, worshipped throughout Egypt, but especially in the Faiyum, and at Gebelein and Koh. The crocodile, which emerged silently and mysteriously from the waters of the lakes and river, was likened to the primeval mound and was thus believed to embody the elemental Kom Ombo in Upper Egypt powers of creation. Although a treacherous creature, it was considered a benefactor of the land, analogous to the Nile whose threatening floodwaters nonetheless ensured the perpetuity of life.

IMAGES 1. Crocodile God (Image #)
Crocodile (Image #1) Paramount Chief Sheku A, T. Fasuluku Sonsiama III of Sandur Chiefdom, Kono District Sierra Leone, West Africa

BA-MBA-A Within the totemic system of the Damby tradition there is a group of people called **Fayee-Tana-tinu. '[fai i ta na ti nu].** The Fayeetanatinnu is gender based totemic system.

This gender based system consists of both males and females. Within the Fayeetanatinnu the males are called 'Bambah'.

The Fayeetanatinnu females are called 'pengusanu'

In all of the Damby totemic systems there is a prohibition against the eating of certain animals. Because the alligator, the crocodile, lizards, and iguana are taboo or prohibited to the 'Bambah' group these animals are not eaten. This taboo does not apply to the female of the Fayeetanatinnu group.

In the Kono language the word for Alligator is 'Bambah'. This is why the word for alligator 'Bambah' is also the word for the name of the male totemic group.

Among the Kono people the Chiefdom is named after the name of a totemic animal. However, although the male can become a chief the Chiefdom is not named after the male totemic animal. Instead, as in the Kono Naming Tradition, the Chiefdom is named after the female totemic group. In this case, the name is 'Pengusa', i.e., female Fayeetanatinnu group.

This chief is the personification of the Great *Sayings of the wise* that was reported in the Holy Bible as spoken by Jesus.

That is, the chief's name, the District he represents, (Pengusa) and his attire, reveals much more than meets the eye. The 'initiatory' declaration or 'initiatory' saying *"ALL POWER HAS BEEN GIVEN TO ME BY 'MY FATHER' . . ."* is revealed as being very close to the saying of the ancient Egyptians; "My heart, of my mother, my heart of

117

transformations" . . . "I am the rudder of the possessor of the two divine faces wherein his beams are seen . . ." (See Budge <u>Egyptian Book of the Dead</u> (1967:439).

This suggests that the source of the 'initiatory' saying of the ancient Serpents of Wisdom of the Kono Branch and the Egyptians is one and the same. It is interesting to note that the word PEN is a prefix to a Kono word for the name of a Pig Damby, females of the Crocodile Damby. Pen is the place where pigs are kept-called the pig pen.

CHAPTER FIVE

Most Famous Pengusah Perssonality:
The Pipeline of the Sandur Leadership

BA-MBA-A Within the totemic system of the Damby tradition there is a group of people called ***Fayee-Tana-tinu.*** **'[fai i ta na ti nu].** The Fayeetanatinnu is gender based totemic system.

This gender based system consists of both males and females. Within the Fayeetanatinnu the males are called 'Bambah'

The Fayeetanatinnu females are called 'pengusanu'

In all of the Damby totemic systems there is a prohibition against the eating of certain animals. Because the alligator, the crocodile, lizards, and iguana are taboo or prohibited to the 'Bambah' group these animals are not eaten. This taboo does not apply to the female of the Fayeetanatinnu group.

In the Kono language the word for Alligator is 'Bambah'. This is why the word for alligator 'Bambah' is also the word for the name of the male totemic group.

Among the Kono people the Chiefdom is named after the name of a totemic animal. However, although the male can become a chief the Chiefdom is not named after the male totemic animal. Instead, as in the Kono Naming Tradition, the Chiefdom is named after the female totemic group. In this case, the name is 'Pengusa', i.e., female Fayeetanatinnu group.

This chief is the personification of the Great *Sayings of the wise* that was reported in the Holy Bible as spoken by Jesus.

That is, the chief's name, the District he represents, (Pengusa) and his attire, reveals much more than meets the eye. The 'initiatory' declaration or 'initiatory' saying *"ALL POWER HAS BEEN GIVEN TO*

ME BY 'MY FATHER' . . ." is revealed as being very close to the saying of the ancient Egyptians; "My heart, of my mother, my heart of transformations" . . . "I am the rudder of the possessor of the two divine faces wherein his beams are seen . . ." (See Budge Egyptian Book of the Dead (1967:439).

This suggests that the source of the 'initiatory' saying of the ancient Serpents of Wisdom of the Kono Branch and the Egyptians is one and the same. It is interesting to note that the word PEN is a prefix to a Kono word for the name of a Pig Damby, females of the Crocodile Damby. Pen is the place where pigs are kept-called the pig pen.

SIR MILTON MARGAI: THE KONO PRIMOGENITURE

Historically, until now almost everyone in Sierra Leone thought that Sir Milton Margai was a Mende. However, let's see what Mr.; T. S Bona has to say on the matter.

According Bona, ". . . .

"The **third** and by no means less important event was the Government's decision to post a Medical Doctor to the Kono District to cure and arrest the spread of an epidemic of skin diseases (yaws, etc.) which had raged in French Guinea and spread south to Koinadugu and Kono Districts.

The young Medical Doctor posted to Kono was no less a person than the late Dr. Milton Margai, and was stationed at Kayima, Fasuluku's home town.

The posting of Dr. Margai to Kono and above all his stationing at Kayima proved invaluable to Fasuluku's, Sandor and: to Kono in purely, from the tribal and ethnic point of view, it was a welcome act of providence, indeed a moral booster.

Interestingly enough, Dr. Margai's paternal grandfather Bangai Margai was in fact a Kono from a small village in the very heart of Fasuluku's Sandor, who had so journeyed to the south and settled in the Banda country amongst the Sherbro-Mendis.

He had led these peace-loving people against their more aggressive northern neighbors, the Kpaa-Mendis and was later recognized as chief of the Banda people.

For all practical purposes he had himself become a Mendi. Bangai Margai was never able to return to his native Sandor. He had Christianized and educated his children, and one of them Milton Margai, had become a very successful businessman.

The young Medical Doctor was the businessman's son, who by a merciful act of providence had been posted to work in the land of his forebears.

As Dr. Margai recounted to a small group of Konos at the Bo School in the early forties, his going to Kayima to serve as a Medical Doctor was a great act of providence reuniting him with his ancestral root.

It was a home going of a kind.

Sandor was the home of his emigrant grandfather with which neither he nor any of his uncles, brothers and sisters had had any prior contact.

He was **blood and bones a Kono**, and yet not of Kono.

Kono in general and Kayima in particular would have marveled and thrilled his simple and honest grandfather. It was a spiritual home going and he plunged into his task with missionary zeal.

Both the chief and the doctor warmed into each other's heart. With the chief's active assistance, the young medical doctor soon traced his roots to a small village in the very heart of Sandor and they paid a joint visit there.

The timing of the posting of Dr. Margai to this part of the new Protectorate could not have been more opportune not only to Fasuluku's but also to Sander, Kono and to the Central Administration.

To Fasuluku, it was barely a little over 10 years after the unfortunate Teya skirmish and from the beginning of his administration he was determined to re-unite his people and divert their attention from the incidents of Teya.

The Medical Doctor, who happily was his own kith and kin, drew him into the affairs of the Administration of health in his chiefdom. Kayima was made a health centre and a sanitary inspector was posted there.

With the help of the Medical Officer who was also in charge of Health and Sanitation a new Kayima village was planned and laid out; and up until today it is one of the cleanest villages in the whole country.

The American Missionaries had already had a Primary school at Kayima, which received great support from both Fasuluku and Dr. Margai. This

School itself became a feeder to the American Central School at Jaiama Nimikore.

To Sandor, Kono and the central government, the timing of the posting of Dr. Margai to Kayima: could not have been more correct and beneficial. It was a little over twenty years after the declaration of the Protectorate, and the British Administrators were determined to give a firm base to their administration which had a poor and unfortunate beginning

They wanted to demonstrate to the people that the new colonial administration was not only concerned with maintaining law and order and collecting taxes from towns and hamlets, but that it had a serious touch of humanity in it in that, it was concerned with the health and sanitation of its subject people.

It had posted to the Kono District, a youthful, industrious and highly trained native African medical doctor.

The government's move proved to be even more popular when the Konos learnt later on that the medical doctor was in fact the grandson of a local boy who had adventured to the south and lived and prospered amongst the Mendes.

He was not only a Kono, but now an emissary of and no mean bridge between the government and the people of Kono. He was also an emissary of the Mendes who up to the turn of the last century, had been warring against the Konos.

The courage and indeed purposefulness of Dr. Margai to have accepted that posting to Kayima in the mid twenties to this century must be commented on even in passing.

Which of our medical doctors even today, would accept being posted to Kayima away from the cinemas, club land and all the attractions of modern life?

By the mid twenties, Kayima was certainly outside the beaten track, and Dr. Margai trekked either on foot or on hammocks firstly to Panguma (a distance of 80 odd miles), and later on to Gandorhun (a distance of 60 miles) to receive medical stores. Sandor itself was almost impassible, sparsely populated and freely roamed by herds of buffaloes, leopards, elephants and even lions.

The Baffin and Bagbe rivers were as still today, un-bridged and Dr. Margai raced to and from and across these rivers in what are known Crew canoes or dugouts. It was no mean sacrifice.

Indeed great minds think alike. The swift personal attraction between the youthful and energetic chief yearning for action, and the equally youthful, highly trained and disciplined Medico, was immensely advantageous to both men. In Dr. Margai, Fasuluku quickly observed the untold advantages of Western education both to the recipient and to his environs.

The chief therefore resolved to give every support and encouragement to the local Primary School, and persuaded his subjects to educate their children.

He set the example by enrolling almost all of his many brothers and some of his sisters at the local school.

He went further to pay the school fees of most of the pupils at the local school from time to time. He continued to do so even when some of the pupils were promoted to the U.M.C. Central School at Jaiama Nimikero some forty miles away from Kayima.

As far as his immediate family is concerned, there is hardly a son of the late chief Kanjama Sonsiama who did not receive a full secondary school education.

How many chiefs throughout Kono and indeed in Sierra Leone who, after succeeding to the chieftaincy turned round to educate all their brothers and a fair number of their sisters? . . ." FROM TRIBUTE TO P.C. SONSIAMA-FASULUKU I . . . 1998 By T. S. BONA

MORE FISH PERSONALITIES

CHAPTER SIX

Jesus is Head of His Christian Damby

N'YEH-TANATINU: THE FISH TOTEMIC DAMBY

DUMBIA-NU IS THE NAME GIVEN TO SOME MEMBERS OF THE FISH EOTEMIC WHOSE PROHIBITION IS THE CATFISH INCLUDING ALL FISHES. HOWEVER, THE SIGN OF JESUS WAS TILAPIA (a freshwater fish of the cichlid family, introduced and cultivated worldwide. Native to: tropical Africa.
Genus: *Tilapia) WHICH THE KONO CALLS "FOHOH".*

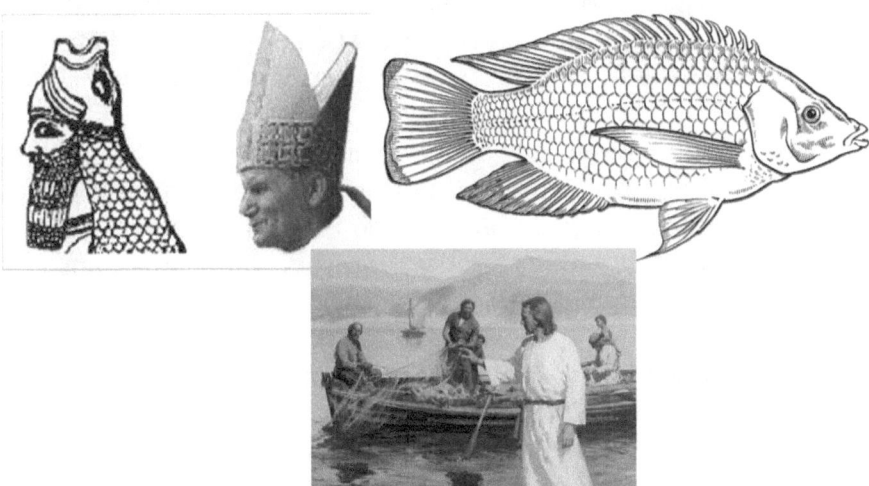

Jesus (the big fish) is also called "son of *Shaphat* or *Sapphias*. The Kono name for *Sapphias* is *Sah-fayah*—meaning the second Sah. Sah-fayah is the name given to the sixth son according to his mother's order of pregnancy. If the name *Sah* represents the first triad of the double triangle and the name Sah-fayah represents the second half, then the name Sah—fayah is representative of the double triangle we commonly call "the star of David". Therefore, the name Sah is depicted by a single fish while the name Sah-fayah is depicted by two fishes.

Jesus the son of Sapphias was a rebel leader during the Roman era. This author stops here on the story of Jesus for it is a corruption of the Ancient Kamitic spiritual system, fragmented and reorganized under fictitious names, symbols and images with a white face.

Dagon or DaKOH is the Kono name which survived in the Uncle-Nephew or Niece Ritual Blessings among the Kono Tribe, the name 'An' was the name of the sun god in Kamit who had plunged into the waters of the womb to be reborn. This may be why the Catholic Church prays to Mary. The Latin name for the ocean or the sea is *'mares or Maris'*. The crocodile 'Sobek' was worshiped around Lake Moeris in ancient Kamet.

The main worship in Babylon was to Dagon, and in Chaldean times the head of the church was the representative of Dagon, he was infallible and people had to kiss his ring and his slipper, and he was also addressed as 'Your Holiness'. He also wore the fish mitre and robes. All these parallel the Catholic Church's Tradition of today. The Catholic Church claims that tradition is a valid source of doctrine. But the Bible states otherwise. See Matthew 15:7 and Isa. 29:13.

The Catholic Church has many traditions taken out of ancient African Traditions which are still performed at their sacred places which they called *Kon-gue-koh, Tambaah-koh or Senge-koh (places of worship* including infant baptism, prayers to the dead and the relics, repetitive prayers with beads, forgiveness of sins, the mass and Sunday worship.

The Catholic Church calls itself the mother of all the Christian churches. Cardinal Ratzinger said in Sept 2000 in "Dominus Iesous" that" It must be always clear that the one, holy catholic and apostolic universal church is not the sister, but the mother of all the churches.

The Catholic Church calls itself the mother of all the Christian churches. Even the pope's staff shows the combinations of the semblances of the African/Kono paramount chiefs' staffs (*Upper and*

Lower Egypt'?) with the cross superimposed on them, symbolizing dominion and control over the African chief's' power to rule over their people.

The Pope's *mitre* also shows four "star of David", the "power symbol" of Judaism. His right hand shows three fingers indicative of the symbol of the "king-makers" in the world, "the serpents of power and wisdom". In his left hand, he held the staff with his 'left fore-finger touching the left thumb' indicative of the "ouroboros serpent" with its tail in its mouth; this is the symbol of 'world domination by the "Learned Elders of Zion", foretold in the Old Testament in guises of the "Promised Land' narratives . . . These symbols tell us that the Pope is not a super human but merely chosen to tell us that there is nothing new in any religious practice. The Pope's decorated attires are adorned with symbols from ancient Egyptian religions. Therefore

They are as old as the African people who are the originators of the symbols.

Symbolism: the use of symbols to invest things with a representative meaning or to represent something abstract by something concrete is covered in a separate volume of these Damby series.

Based on the Kono Damby Tradition, one can make a sound argument that the Catholic Pope is the Damby Head or Damby Mansah of the fish totemic people collectively known as the Catholics or Christians. Here, the fish is Jesus as evidenced by the pope's head dressing or cap. As the pig is covered by mud; the Catholics or Christians are covered by the blood of the "Fish", Jesus. The Pope wears the emblem of the fish on his head to support this claim.

Augustine wrote concerning the fish: "If you combine the initial letters of the five Greek words, which are **Iesous Chreistos Theou Uios Soter**, which means Jesus Christ the Son of God the Savior, they make the word **ICHTHUS**, meaning fish, and the mystic meaning of this noun is Christ, because He had power to exist alive, that is, without sin, *in the bottomless pit of our mortal life*, as in the depths of the sea."

The amphibious 'Oannes' is also associated with the Johannine Christian tradition that reveres Saint John over the other Apostles.

John the submerger or 'baptizer' is Joannes or 'J-OANNNES'. And both the traditional and still popular symbol of Jesus is the fish—more specifically the geometric shape formed by the overlap of two circles at their centre called the *'Vesica Piscis'*—symbolic also of the female labia. This geometric symbol call, the *'Vesica Piscis'*, is depicted in the Kono traditional male name of Pessima.

The word Pessima in the Kono language means, "like a fish", "sign of a fish" or "symbol of a fish" Peh, from the prefix of the word Pessima is name for a tiny fish, The word "sima-ah" means 'similar to', sample of" or 'symbol of' something'. Thus, Peh + Sima-ah, yield "fish symbol . . ."

The word 'Essenes', of which Jesus the 'Nazarene' is thought to have been a member, is derived from the word 'Naaz' or 'Naasenes', a sect revering SOPHIA as the light-bringing 'wisdom' of the serpent (OPHIS. the Kono name for this serpent was Gofoh or Ofoh, which is the origin of the word Ngofoh, meaning magician). Dagon the Fish God of the ancient is depicted in Christianity.

Based on the ancient traditional worship of Dagon, the Pope whose mitre or hat is an exact duplicate of the fish-head hats worn by the High priest of Dagon can be interpreted as the Papal attempt to bring back the old glory of worship of Dagon, thus, I posit a question: is the Pope is a High Priest of Dagon the fish-god of the ancient Hebrews?

NUN OR NUNN

The word *Nun* in Kono means hidden, in other cultures, the word Nun means both fish and growth. The word Nun is still the name of a female devotee of the Christian faith. The earlier Christian representation of the Trinity was three fishes. The Pope's cap is made like a fish-head (*Tilapia or Bonga-head*) The Fish is also one of the eight sacred symbols of Buddha. The dolphin was the sacred fish of Apollo (the Solar Savior) and Neptune, because it was believed that this fish carried shipwrecked sailors to heaven on its back. Thus, the dolphin was chosen by earlier Christians as an emblem of Christ, because the dolphin was regarded as a friend and benefactor of mankind.

In ancient initiatory rituals of the Persians, Greeks and Egyptian mysteries, the priests disguise themselves as a composite creature as symbolizing the different aspects of the human consciousness. For example, the leopard priests of the ancient Egyptians.

CHAPTER SEVEN

Fish Heads

JESUS IS THE PRIMOGENITOR OF HIS CATHOLIC DAMBY BY THE SEA OF GALEALI

Yehowshuwa the son of *Yeewah* stated; [*Matthew 15:7-9*] hypocrites, *well did Ysaias prophesy of you, when he said:" "These people draw near me with their mouths and honor me with their lips; but their hearts hold off and are away from me. "Uselessly do they worship me, for they teach as doctrines the commands of men*

THE POPE, AND THE FISH TOTEMIC GROUPS

Isaiah 29:13-15, wherefore *Yeewah* said, *"Therefore this iniquity and guilt will be to you like a broken section of a high wall bulging out and ready."14" Therefore, behold, I will proceed to do a marvelous work among this people, a marvelous work and a wonder: for the wisdom of their wise shall perish, and the understanding of their prudent shall be hide." 15 ". . . In returning to me and resting in me you shall saved; in quietness and in trusting confidence shall be your strength. But you would not."*

In the mean time, to keep this "Motherhood" position, the Catholic Church made a new move as reported by James Graff, in World Editor . . .

IMAGE # POPE LAID IN-STATE FOR THE JOURNING BACK TO THE HISTORICAL WOMB OF THE OCEAN

According to James Graff, World Editor, the number of married Catholic priests could grow sharply as the result of the Vatican's epochal decision to welcome thousands of disaffected Anglicans and Episcopalians into the Catholic Church.

At press conferences in Rome and London on Tuesday, Vatican officials announced that the Church would set up a special canonical structure that will ease the conversion of members of the Anglican Communion without them having to give up what the Vatican called "the distinctive Anglican spiritual and liturgical patrimony." That means not only a body of prayers and hymns, but also a tradition of married priests and bishops.

"It's a stunning turn of events," says Lawrence Cunningham, theology professor at Notre Dame University. "This decision will allow for many more married clergy in Western churches, and that's going to raise a new question, 'If they can do it, why can't the priests of Rome," says Cunningham. "I can already picture the electronic slugfest on the Internet in coming days and weeks." The Catholic Church already allows clergymen who convert from Protestant denominations to remain married on a case by case basis, and married priests are common in the Eastern Rite, a group that uses Orthodox traditions but is loyal to Rome.

THE AFRICAN CATHOLICS FINALLY SPOKE OUT

"African cardinals denounced the "cultural imperialism" of wealthy countries in their aid, trade and health care policies for Africa, saying Wednesday that the West's promotion of abortion rights and condoms is destroying the continent's moral fabric. African prelates (a high-ranking member of the Christian clergy, e.g.

an abbot, bishop, or cardinal) attending the three-week meeting on the role of the Catholic Church in Africa said their countries needed economic development partnerships that are ***based on trust and fairness, not ones that exploit Africa's natural resources and put conditions on aid.*** *"We want to be helped, but helped in the name of truth, with respect of what we are and what we want for ourselves,"* [***Especially when all the Pope's Symbolic Atares are taken out of Africa***] Cardinal Theodore Adrien **Sarr** of Dakar, Senegal, told a news conference". By JAMES GRAFF, World Editor

PART III

CHAPTER ONE

The Significance of Men and Women in Both Ancient Hebrew and Ancient Kono Communities

THE POSITION OF THE ANCIENT WOMEN

When a woman was young, she belonged to her father.

When married, she belonged to her husband.

When she was widowed, she belonged to her oldest son.

When she was old, widowed, and childless and had no father, or no male relatives, or possessed any of the property that might have belonged to the family, she was helpless. She could not inherit any of the property that might have belonged to the family. She could not make a living. She had to live on charity and be an object of pity or scorn. Thus, it was a disgrace to be in such a position.

She was restricted to roles of little or no authority.

She was largely confined to her father's or husband's home.

She was considered to be inferior to men and to be under the authority of men, including her father before marriage or her husband, son, or brother afterwards.

The importance of the male image and the male position was so deeply embedded in the ancient Kono concept that this particular belief is in existence today and as strong as it was in the past. For example, no Kono woman has any strong governmental position. She cannot be chief or a member of parliament. She cannot be a president or a prime minister of the country in the Kono community. In fact, to protect this belief, the position of the matrilineal uncle is made so strong that he has the same rights as the mother and more rights than the father over his nieces and nephews. Secondly, there is a prayer that says: a woman without a husband is the delight of the village, meaning that she is prostitute. They equated this with the concept of a chicken without a coup, which they considered a wild fowl.

THE POSITION OF THE ANCIENT MEN

He could have more than one wife.

He could treat women servants as though they were wives except that they have no usual honor, respect, and legal status that legal wives have.

The women could play the role of his concubines and handmaidens.

He has the rights and the power of the levirate choice under the levirate law unlike a woman.

Significance of Daughters

The problems can be the following: They need to be taken care of, and her only worth is in finding a man who could take care of her.

Significance of Sons

The significance of sons can include the following: They are the pride of the family, the inheritors of property, the workers of the farm, and the winners of renown in war and council and in great deeds. So too, he can be anything a woman cannot be.

WOMEN AND THE MESSAGE OF THE BIBLE AS UNDERSTOOD AND USED BY MEN IN THE SERVICE OF GOD

I. A GENERAL STATEMENT

If you want my view in compressed form, it is as follows: I believe that God has laid the burden of leading his people upon men. From Genesis through Revelation, God consistently laid that burden upon men not women. I further believe that the same principles that call forth godly men to lead the nation of Israel are the same principles that call forth godly men to lead the Christian church. I believe those same principles are at work in the marriage relationship, which is why the husband is the head of his own home.

Nonetheless, I wonder what Jesus' ministry would have been without the note the taking ability of his mother—not his stepfather, the carpenter, the external or physical or should I say 'the bread-winner' laborer like Adam. His father, Joseph, undoubtedly must have helped him tremendously, but the Bible is silent on this. Therefore, I do not believe in **egalitarian** leadership the view that men and women should share equally in leading the people of God. Such a view, in my opinion, is unbiblical and wrong. It is a violation of the biblical pattern and an unnecessary compromise with the Spirit of this Age.

Man and Woman	
↓	
Division of Labor	
Man	Physical Work
Woman	Spiritual: Child Bearing

II. Another Look at Genesis 1-3

What do we find when we go to the first pages of the Bible? It is crucial to answer this question because the pattern for leadership is laid down in the first three chapters of Genesis. Let me list some of the obvious principles.

"Division of Labor".

1. Men and women share equally in bearing the image of God.
2. Men and women are both given the command to subdue the earth 1:28.
3. As the "king of creation," man is created first. 2:15, as a gardener, external leadership in the physical realm.
4. The command to rule the earth was first given to man. 2:15

5. Woman is created later to meet the need of man's loneliness 2:18
6. The woman is created as a "Helper", one who completes what is lacking. This does not mean she is a weak helper, but an inner leader as in spirituality. 2:18
7. To signify the close relationship, the woman is created from the man's body. 2:22. God separated the two opposites but equal beings involved in their individual ministries.
8. To signify his leadership position, the man names the woman. 2:23 we all have pet names for persons or objects of our affection. This is the reason—Jesus—God has many names.
9. The woman sins first, being deceived by the Serpent. 3:6.
10. The man sins deliberately. He bears the ultimate responsibility for the fall. 3:6. Intentional sin caused the fall.
11. As a result of the Fall, the relationship between man and woman is now changed. Establishment of gender role is born.

    A. She will suffer in childbirth 3:16a while the man continues to be the gardener, but the earth would not obey him.
    B. She will suffer in relation to her husband 3:16b

Where does all this leave us? I quote now from the "Affirmations" found in the "Danvers Statement" as published by the Council on Biblical Manhood and Womanhood:

1. Both Adam and Eve were created in God' image, equal before God as persons they were distinct in their manhood and womanhood.
2. Distinctions in masculine and feminine roles are ordained by God as part of the created order, and should find an echo in every human heart.
3. Adam's headship in marriage was established by God before the fall, and was not the result of sin. It was a mere division of labor in God's Kingdom on earth.

4. However, the Fall introduced distortions into the relationships between men and women:

In the home, the husband's loving, humble leadership tends to be displaced by domination or passivity; the wife's intelligent, willing submission tends to be replaced by usurpation or servility.

In the church, sin inclines men toward a worldly love of power or an *abdication* of spiritual responsibility, and inclines women to resist limitations on their roles or to neglect the use of their gifts in appropriate ministries.

Such a view is not based upon any supposed male superiority or any supposed female inferiority. As Genesis 1 makes it clear, men and women are both made in the image of God. They are equal in worth and dignity. They are equal in bearing the image of God. As humanity comes from the hand of the Creator, it comes as male and female. Adam failed in his leadership position by trading his birthright for the forbidden fruit—an apple, a food. Likewise, Esau who traded his birthright for a bowl of red soup, a food.

Moreover, equal does not mean identical. Nor does equal mean interchangeable. As Adam and Eve are created, they complement each other; they do not replace each other. Adam is a man with a 'dangling'; Eve is a woman with a 'bleeding hole'. From the beginning, there are vast differences between the two, differences which are much more than simple biology. Adam is called by God to be a manly man; Eve is called by God to be a womanly woman. Adam is masculine; Eve is feminine. They are equal but different. Adam is a gardener for God, Eve is the incubator or womb-man; both were fired out of the garden.

Adam is the leader in the Garden of Eden. He is the 'pipe' layer. The woman is taken from his side, not him from her side. He names her; she doesn't name him. All of God's conversations are with Adam, not with Eve. Why? Because as the theologians have told us for generations, Adam is the responsible head of the human race, God holds him accountable for the entrance of sin into the world. If this the case, why did God punish Eve?

There is a divine pattern of leadership in the very beginning of the Bible. Adam is the "king of creation," the head of his wife, and the person held responsible for the fall. Most importantly, it must be said here again that the fall does not establish Adam's leadership. That was established long before the fall. Adam is the leader from the very beginning. But he failed as a leader and as man. We see this today in our society—homosexuality, men assuming woman's role. Men, even male preachers are now talking of being in trivial—child labor—when will this stop?

THE SIGNIFICANCE OF GENESIS IN I TIMOTHY 2

We come now to the crux of the issue. In I Timothy 2:8-15, Paul who was blinded in order to become an Apostle of Jesus lays down certain principles concerning the respective roles of men and women in God's house, the local church:

1. Men are to be godly models of prayer. 8.
2. Women are to dress modestly. 9 As if they came to dress man-God-Jesus, but the tomb was empty—nobody home.
3. Women are to adorn themselves with good works and have no other God.
4. Women are to receive biblical instruction with a submissive spirit from men. 11
5. Women are not to teach men or to exercise authority over men in the local church, yet the church is the seed of the woman. 12.

What does this last point mean? It means at least this much. Women—even godly women—are not to exercise spiritual authority over men in the local church. Furthermore, they are not to be in the position of authoritatively teaching the Word of God to men—whether from the pulpit or (I would judge) in a Sunday school classrooms. This means (at the very least) that a woman may not serve as a pastor or an elder in a local church.

However, be reminded that Paul had a vision and kicked out the 12 disciples from Jesus like he kicked women to the back seat in local churches—yes, indeed, he had a vision to Damascus alright.

Paul goes on to give two reasons for this teaching:

1. The order of creation: Adam was created first.
2. The order of the Fall: Eve was deceived; Adam sinned deliberately. 14

   It is very, very important to notice that these reasons are not cultural. They have nothing to do with the situation at Ephesus, nothing to do with whether the Ephesians' women were rebellious or ill-educated, nothing to do with the status of women in the first century. These reasons are trans-cultural. They apply as much to us in Kaikudu, as they did to the church in Ephesus. It is still true that Adam was created first. It is still true that Eve was deceived. By their nature, these facts do not change. Thus, any attempt to explain any passage in I Timothy 2 on the basis of culture will not work. Paul bases his teaching not on any local situation, but on timeless and eternal principles rooted in Genesis 1-3. We do not have the option of changing or diluting these principles in any way.

Finally, we ought to notice Paul's promise to women in verse 15. "But women will be kept safe through childbirth, if they continue in faith, love and holiness with propriety." This verse has been interpreted in three primary ways:

1. Those women will physically be kept safe through childbirth.
2. Those women will be spiritually saved through the birth of Christ. (They were disciples.)
3. Those women will be preserved from insignificance through fulfilling her role in the family. She multiplies membership through child-bearing.

Along with many other commentators, Douglas Moo opts for the third view. For him:

We think it is preferable to view verse 15 as designating the circumstances in which Christian women will experience . . .

> their salvation—in maintaining as priorities those key roles that Paul, in keeping with Scripture elsewhere, highlights: being faithful, helpful wives, raising children to love and reverence God, managing the household . . . This I not to say, of course, that women cannot be saved unless they bear children. The women with whom Paul is concerned in this paragraph are all almost certainly married, so that he can mention one central role—bearing and raising children—as a way of designating appropriate female roles generally. Probably Paul makes this point because the false teachers were claiming that women could really experience what God had for them only if the abandoned the home and . . .

However, the Kono females of the crocodile or alligator clan are only prohibited from eating the pig, swine, boar, or hog. The reason for this may be lost in history, or as matter of clan secrecy is fully known only to the clan members. Thus, the link continuous and links us to the Zodiac Star Systems of which I may say:

America fills the promise made to the children of God before the Magdalenian drew the Cows Coming Home to the Leo Cancer Boundary in the cave at Lascaux over 17,000 years ago. All of the aurochs have been taken down from the sky by the rationalizations of man, but one bull still holds her ground. She is the bull of my Mother, and she still wears the seven-pointed crown upon her head. And she still stands stretching the cord of the magical wisdom of God. Her light rises above the very door that the angry arrogance of Islam attempted to close. After they took down the SA at New York City, Seshat revealed it within the great pyramid as the essence of her magic. The back of every dollar bill has the hidden SA messages of the greatest stories ever told. "Think!" she shouted from the heavens and said to the children in the new promised land of the ages.

Nonetheless, as long as the children keep their hands to the plow and connect the dots, there is no telling where the winding path of truth's journey will pass through the wilderness. It must eventually lead to heaven above, where a place has been prepared for the future mothers of God. For that reason, any who would pursue heavenly desires should take the guideline for dating ancient astronomical data and eat it up. It may appear to be the refuse of ruminating beasts (pigs), but it may contain the manna from heaven in the shadow of a compassionate, conservative creation waiting to be reincarnated within a loving heart through the door of a reopened mind.

PART IV

CHAPTER ONE

The Gods of Ancient Egypt are Still the Gods Depicted in Kono Damby Tradition

KONDAI-KODAI-EH: A Kono word for Butterfly

The butterfly is also known as "Psyche", a beautiful maiden with wings of opalescent light, symbolizing the human soul because of the stages it passes through to unfold its power of flight. *The butterfly goes through three divisions of enfoldment; this parallels the three degrees of the Mystery Schools' stages of knowledge* which are seen as consummating the enfoldment of man by giving him the emblematic wings (*the marks of poneh*) by which he may soar to the skies. The butterfly is emblem of metamorphosis.

UNCIRCUMCISED MALE.

BEE-YEE-KAMIN-NEH: this is a Kono word for unregenerate male.

For the Kono, this male is ignorant and helpless who needs to grow into manhood, thus he is symbolized by the stages between *ovum* and larva, the disciple seeking truth and dwelling in meditation by *the second* stage, from larva to pupa, at which time the insect enters its Chrysalis (the tomb or womb) of the mysteries); the *Third* stage, from *pupa* to imago (wherein the perfect butterfly comes forth), typifies the unfolded enlightened soul of the initiate rising from the tomb of his base nature. Here, the Kono word Kama (ancient Egypt) and Kama-da-ah, (the gate of ancient Egypt), is very significant for the Kono males understanding of the Poro initiation society he is so proud of.

149

Remember that in the days of Biblical Joshua (Kono, *Jeh-soh-a-ah-yor*) according to the Bible; the sun did stand still. ***"Sun, Stand Thou Still Upon Gideon; And Thou, Moon, In the Valley Of Ajalo"***

(Keseh or Kese is a Hebrew word for the full-moon but a Kono word for vagina)

CHAPTER TWO

Animal Gods of Egypt

The earliest Egyptians like many modern African Traditions seem to have represented their gods by means of *fetishes:* something, especially an inanimate object, that is revered or worshiped because it is believed to have magical powers or be animated by a spirit which they carried about as tribal standards—feathers, flags, arrows, stuffed or modeled birds and animals, even fossilized mollusks.

Nonetheless, as the years rolled by, these dead forms were supplemented with living ones chosen from among the Nile valley's tributaries vast profusion of fauna—*crocodiles, jackals, lions, falcons, vultures, beetles, ibises, baboons, bulls, rams, geese*, and many more—each, like the inanimate fetishes, associated with a particular tribe or locale.

That the Egyptians were still thinking in these terms even into the dynastic (The Damby Tradition) era is confirmed by the very names of the early kings of the Archaic Period—Scorpion, Catfish, Falcon, Snake—as well as by their ceremonial palettes and mace; **ceremonial staff of office:** a stick or rod, usually with an ornamental head, carried by officials on ceremonial occasions as a symbol of authority, e.g., serpent heads dresses, which clearly show the tribal standards being carried into battle and the totemic deities fighting on behalf of their clients.

BIRD TOTEMIC OR BIRD DAMBY: This group is called *Kondaih-tana-tinu, meaning those who do not eat birds and chickens even the particular bird prohibition which is manikin bird.*

Nubian King Tahaqa, who the ancient Kono knew as Takamah is kneeling before in of the golden Horus.

Kondaih is the kono word for a bird, the prohibition here is the manikin which in Kono is *Soyaineh.*

BIRDS' USEFULNESS AS UNDERSTOOD BY THE HOLY BIBLE

BIRDS were listed among the first created living Creatures on earth, coming into existence on the fifth creative 'day' along with water creatures, *see Gen. 1:20. In Psalm 148: 1, 10* called on the 'winged' birds to praise god. Birds naturally obey this divined command by their very structure and their complex design. A single bird may have from 1000 to more than 20,000 feathers. Nonetheless, each feather is composed of a shaft from which branch out hundreds of 'barbs' forming on inner "web", each barb containing hundred smaller barbules and hook-lets.

The Holy Bible told us about what part Noah played with regards to preserving the bird species, he placed them in the 'ark' two x two

(2x2) or by pairs according to their kinds. Well, you know the rest of the story.

At the end of the 'global-flood 'Noah offered clean flying creatures or birds along with other animals as sacrifices, (Gen. 8:18-20). From here on, God has ordained/thereby allowing birds as inclusion into human diet as long as the blood was not eating.

However, *Gen. 9:1-4;* compare *Le. 7:26; and 17:13.* The 'cleaning-ness' certain birds at that time was established and thereby evidencing some divine indication of acceptance for sacrifice. From the Bible's perspective regarding birds as food, none of the birds were declared as 'unclean' until the introduction of the Mosaic Code/Law *(Le 11:13-19, 46, 47; 20:25; De. 14:11-20.* even then, the factors determining which birds were declared ceremonially 'unclean' are not clearly stated in the Bible.

This is an indication that most of the ancient Hebrew diet laws were copied from ancient Egyptians, the fore-runners of the Hebrew religious system. Moses was not only an Egyptian Prince brought-up on the laps of the Egyptian Priests, he was also, an adept in the Egyptian Mystery Religious belief system rooted in African concepts.

Furthermore, Islam and Christianity both are derived from the Hebrews who got theirs from the Egyptians/African.

Therefore, while most of the so called declared were birds of pray or scavengers, not all of them were.

However, these prohibitions were lifted after following the establishment of the New Covenant, as God made "evident to Peter by a vision. ***See Act 10: 9-15.***

Another factor in the identification of the birds specifically named in the Bible presents a difficult task in certain cases. The lexicographers were guided by the meaning of the name, since this was usually descriptive, by indications in the context as to the birds' habit and habitat; and by observation of the birds known to be found in the Bible-lands. In many cases the names are believed to be **"*Onomatopoeic"*** that is, meaning the sound produced by the bird. The Kono tradition called the owl **"*Buu-u"*** based on the sound made by the owl.

An image of scavenger birds gather around a carcass was one of the images used in the Bible as the basis for an ominous warning to an enemy (1Sa. 17:44-46), and constantly formed part of divinely inspired prophetic warnings to the nation of Israel and rulers *(De.28:26; 1Ki. 14:11; 21:24; Jer. 7:33; 15:3)*; as well as to foreign nations. These images were seen in the Kono District during the *Blood Diamond War* in Sierra Leone. See *(Isa. 18:1, 6; Eze 29:5; 32:24)*.

Therefore, Jehovah/the Biblical use to execute judgment was figuratively represented by the 'birds of prey' *(Isa. 46:11)*. Desolation of a city or land was depicted by its becoming the habitat of certain birds of solitary nature *(Isa. 13:19-21)*, compare *Rev. (18:2)* or by the disappearance of all life. *(Jer 4:25-27; 9:10; 12:4; Ho 4:3; Zep 1:3)*. The proclamation calling all the birds to gather to feast on the dead bodies of Gog of Magog and his crowd *(Eze 39:1-4, 17-21)* is parallel by that recorded in Revelation in which the bodies of national rulers and their armies became food for 'all the birds that fly in midheaven' as a result of the executional work of Christ Jesus as King-*Rev 19:11-21*; to be contrasted with God's comforting words to his people, *at Ho 2:18-20.*

The using or worshipping of birds as representing the true God was prohibited to the nation of Israel (De 4:15-17) but was prominent among the so called pagan nations, particularly in Egypt. (Rom: 23). Hundreds of bird mummies have been discovered in Egyptian tombs, principally of birds such as the falcon, vulture, and the ibis, all of which were sacred among the Egyptians. Egyptian hieroglyphics contain some 22 different bird signs.

Clearly, as you can see the Christians sort of believe in the divinity of the Birds as the Kono Damby do. However, the Christians do not call this belief and use of the birds as *'fetish'* but call the African attitude toward the same as fetish.

According to the Bible, at the time of Jesus' baptism, and subsequent "anointing" by God's Holy Spirit who was caused to appear 'in the bodily shape of a dove'. The dove's visible descent upon Jesus being similar to the fluttering descent as it approaches its perch. (Lu. 3:22; Matt 3:16; Mark 1:10; Job 1:2-34). It was an apt symbol, in view of its characteristic innocence-Matt 10:16.

Furthermore, even though birds, i. e., doves were used as sacrificial purposes as indicated by their being sold by those pursuing commercial activities at the temple in Jerusalem, although the terms of the behavior was not viewed as fetish.

Doves have strong wings and able to fly long distant in search of food; and are swift enough to escape or elude most enemies. (*Psalm 55: 6-8*). On the other-hand, doves are very trusting of humans and as a result they are easily entrapped or snared with a net. Therefore, apostate Ephraim foolishly placing his confidence first in Egypt and then in Assyria, was likened to a "simple-minded dove" due to be caught in a net. (*Ho7:11, 12*).

Remember, here that Jesus was able to gain the trust of Mathew and other first disciples by telling them where to cast their fishing nets.

Hence Jesus, in warning his disciples against wolf-like opposers counseled them to be not only "innocent as doves" but also cautious as serpents. (*Matt 10:16*). If the "inocence" of doves can be equated with "wisedom" of a "serpents", then, who was the being that caused the dove to land on the head of Jesus calling him "my belved Son in whom I am well pleased, to the point of anointing him during the cause of his baptism? Who was the being that gave the warning asking them to be like the dove and the serpent in their daily life styles?

Therefore, the Kono believe in the powers of the divinity of animals, such as birds and serpents go far beyond human created "his-story".

KONDENU

The bird totemic groups are known as *Kondenu in the Kono Tradition*. However, the bird prohibition is the manikin bird, this Kono call **Soyaineh**, which was known in ancient Egypt as the *Ben-ben bird*. The Konde groups who are prohibited from eating all birds including chickens are few in number, but are scattered all over the Kono chiefdoms. The Kondenu do not inter-marry, at least, in the ancient times. However, they do now.

THE BENU (BENNU

According to the ancient Egyptians, the Benu which the Kono call *Soyaineh* and a Damby totemic animal is Osiris. In essence, the Benu was considered a manifestation of the resurrected Osiris.

As an aspect of Atum, the Benu bird was also said to have flown over the waters of Nun before the original creation. According to this tradition, the bird came to rest *on a rock* from which its cry broke the primeval silence and this determined what was and what was not to be in the unfolding creation.

The Benu, according to ancient Egyptian mythology, was also believed to be the ***ba of Re***, and by Egypt's Late Period, the hieroglyphic sign depicting the bird was used to write the name of this sun god. During the Middle Kingdom, it was said that the Benu of Re was the means by which Atum came into being in the primeval water.

Like the sun god, the Benu's own birth is attributed to self generation. A mythological papyrus of the 21st Dynasty provides a vignette of a heart-amulet and scarab beetle near to which stand the Benu, which is described as "the one who came into being by 'himself". It was believed to constantly rise and renewed itself just like the sun, and was called the *"lord of jubilees"*. The Benu Bird was said to rise each morning and appears under the form of the rising sun, and was supposed to shine upon the world from the top of the famous Persia tree in Heliopolis from where it renews itself.

This may be the origin or source of the concept of bird's long life, which was later transferred and identified with the Greek phoenix, which also renews itself from a fiery death like the sun rising at dawn. In fact, it may have been the prototype for the phoenix, and there may well be an etymological connection between the two birds' names, though certainly there are distinct differences between myths surrounding them.

The bird was primarily associated with Atum and Re, but inevitably, its connection with rebirth came to associate it also with Osiris. In quoting from the Book of the Dead, Wallis Budge quotes a passage that reads, "I go in like the Hawk, and I come forth like the Bennu, the Morning Star (i.e., the planet Venus) of Ra. "I am the Bennu which is in Heliopolis". He continued that the scholion on this passage expressly informs us that the Benu is Osiris. In essence, the Benu was considered a manifestation of the resurrected Osiris.

To Herodotus, the Benu bird lives for 500 years before building a nest of aromatic boughs and spices which it then set ablaze and was consumed within the inferno. From this conflagration, a new Benu bird raises who, after embalming its father's ashes, flew with the ashes to Heliopolis where it deposited the ashes on the altar of the temple of Re. In this respect, the Benu parallels the Greek Phoenix that is also reborn from its own ashes.

The iconography of the Benu was displayed a temple of Re at Heliopolis where the Benu bird first served as a symbol of solar deities and it; according to the Pyramid Texts, represented Atum. Sometimes the Benu bird was depicted as a gray heron with long legs and beak, and a two-feather crest growing form the back of its head. From here, the bird surmounted a stylized ben-ben stone as a symbol of the great solar god association with Osiris.

However, it was also sometimes represented in the sacred willow of that god. In addition, it was also sometimes, depicted wearing the _Atef Crown_ in its aspect as Osiris. In at least, one the sarcophagus of the Divine Adoratrice of Amun, Ankhnesneferibre, and now in the British Museum, the Benu is imagined as perched on a sacred willow tree in the temple. Furthermore, the Benu was also depicted in a hybrid form with the head of a man. Classically, the Benu bird is described as being as large as an eagle, with red and gold (solar or flame-colored) plumage.

This most likely led to the concept of its long life, later identifying it with the Greek phoenix which also renewed itself from a fiery death like the sun rising at dawn. In fact, it may have been the prototype for the phoenix, and there may well be an etymological connection between the two birds' names, though certainly there are distinct differences between myths surrounding them.

A bird was frequently depicted in the vignettes of the netherworld books as well as on heart amulets and other objects, particularly those of a funerary nature. When carved on the back of a heart-scarab and buried with the dead, it is a symbol of anticipated rebirth in the netherworld and ensures that the heart does not fail in the examination of past deeds in the Hall of the Two Truths (judgment of the dead). In the Book of the Dead there are formulae to transform the deceased into the Great Benu. Here, the deceased says, "I am the Benu, the soul of Ra, and the guide of the gods in the Duat." In another verse, he says, "I am pure. My purity is the purity of the Great Benu which is in the city *of Suten-henen*." The word *of Suten-henen* in the Kono language means "the birth-place is here . . .", hence the etymological meaning is the same as the ancient Egyptian meaning.

BIRD-WORSHIP

Wallis Budge tells us that "the sanctuary of the Bennu was the sanctuary of Ra and <u>Osiris</u>, and was called **Het Benben**, i.e., the 'House of the Obelisk' . . ." However, almost nothing else is known about the worship of the most ancient of Egyptian icons.

KONDAIH, (bird) with WORSHIPER, of the bird form of ancient Egyptian Horus, this is the origin of the bird Damby Tradition among the Kono. There are people in the Kono tribe with a word or nane, Kondaih (bird) added to theirs birth names, e.g., *Saa Kondaih, (Saa-bird),—or Saa kondaih_nyaneh, (Saa bird nest),* depicting a totemic believes in animal-bird ancestors in Damby Animals

The word, *Kon-daih* is the Kono word for the word bird. The Kono family whose totem is the bird or any kind of birds is collectively called **Kon-daih-tana-ti-nu,** meaning people with *bird Totemic Prohibition. Kon-daih-tana-ti-nu are also prohibited from eating chicken.*

Thoth with Writing Tablet: The Egyptian god of law, arbitration, science and writing, the ibis-headed god Thoth, is represented here as the observer, and the creator of written word as he was often revered. He is formed as though he is taking notes with his chisel and tablet, with his dark eyes staring past his writing to that which he exists beyond.

Ibis Headed Thoth: Thoth the ibis headed was the Egyptian god of wisdom and writing. Thoth conceived himself at the beginning of time, and was the scribe to the gods and husband of Ma`at. He recorded the results of the weighing of a spirits heart against the feather of Ma`at. He is also credited with the invention of astronomy, geometry and medicine

HOURS

The word Hour has not changed in centuries. The word denotes the name of an Egyptian sun god Horus. The image of Horus is sometimes portrayed as *hawk, wearing the solar disc*. He was the rising sun that flew up into the sky, and known as *Horus of the horizon*. In the early days, when one wanted to know what time it was, meaning where the sun was at a particular time of the day, one would ask, "what *Horus* is it?" (Where is *Horus* now?). Today we say, "What *hour* is it?" Or what is the time?

Like the ancient Egyptians, the ancient Kono people attributed the ability of birds to leave the earth and fly aloft toward the source of light symbolizes them as emblems of inspiration, purity and beauty. Thus, wings are used in most rituals and suggestion of transcendence, or the vehicle of the soul. Sometime first born male children in the Kono culture are called Sahr with the name Kondaih, meaning bird added to the word Sahr to yield Sahr-Kondaih.

Birds in ancient Kono Tradition were regarded as messengers of the spirits at the *Kon-go-eh-Ko-oh, (a place of worship at the base of the sacred Mountains), these also includes other* spirits and nature goods inhabiting the spirits of hills, mountains, and other high places. The rationale here is that by nature, birds live in the branches of the sacred forests. However, they were not worshipped; they were regarded as objects that the gods speak through to humans.

BIRDS AND REPTILES AS EMBLEMS OF DIVINITY.

The ancients believe that animals like birds and reptiles had certain spiritual and transcendental truths concealed from the profane.

To the ancient mystery schools, the composite animals and birds simply represent various forces working in the invisible world.

Birds symbolize gravity and levitation capabilities as outlined below.

BIRDS

To the ancients birds were symbols of the vital breath. Therefore, they depicted them as emblems of human as well as divine attributes. For this and other reasons, birds were therefore, included in religious and philosophic symbols of both the ancients and Christianity, for example,

Cruelty	—	Buzzard
Courage	—	Eagle
Self-Sacrifice	—	Pelican
Pride	—	Peacock

THE PHOENIX;

Made its nest of incense and flames.

UNICORN: had the body of a horse (an animal that dares the wind), the feet of an elephant (*the totemic animal of the Kono Kama-tana-tinu*) and the tail of a *wild boar (the emblem of the pengusa Damby women)*

THE PELICAN: the hermetic animal emblem of the pelican feeds her young from its own breast or heart. Note here that the *Yawanneh* females do not eat *fu-u* or drink the *fu-u-gb-u*, the endosperm of the—palm tree often found floating in palm wines as they are the product of the heart of the palm tree. *See* THE TANA OF YAYANNENU below.

GRAVITATION: deals with certain natural laws in the material and in the spiritual world. The impulse toward the center of spirituality naturally draws one in the center towards the source.

LEVITATION: like gravitation, it also has its own natural laws—the impulse toward the center. *Birds* seem to neutralize the effects of *gravity*. Thus, considered as partakers of a nature superior to other terrestrial creation and their feathers having a sustaining power, the ancient depicts them as symbols of divinity, courage and accomplishment.

Thus, the American Indian uses the feathers of eagle as part of the ceremonial outfits. For the same reason, the, angels are fitted with wings; and as messengers of gods, and man they live in the air, Middle Kingdom, between heaven and earth.

SIMBI_YE; A KONO WORD FOR EAGLE: A bird of Hermes or the Hermetic Symbol of sulphur and represents mysterious fire of Scorpio, the Sign of the Zodiac and a gate of the mystery. It is one of the three symbols of Scorpio, the eagle like the *Goat* of Mendes was an emblem of the theurgic *(the supposed intervention of supernatural powers in the affairs of humans)*, ART AND THE SECRET OF TRANSMUTED SCORPIO FIRE INTO SPIRITUAL LIGHT—FIRE OF THE GODS.

THUNDERBIRD: According to American Indian legend, it lives above the clouds, the flapping of its wings causes the rumbling that comes with the storms. The flash from its eyes are lightning.

GBAI-YA-GBAI-YAH: a Kono word for Hawks; Hawks signify immortality which they carry in their claws, are the emblem of the liberated soul of the dead.

TEH-KONEH; a Kono word for the cock—rooster; A rooster is a phallic symbol sacred to the sun and represents watchfulness and as a defense. The Greeks like the Africans sacrifice roosters to the gods, at the time of entering the secret societies. The rituals are performed and the fowl is killed, cooked and all members eat while some of the foods are scattered on the ground near or on sacred areas on the ground for formal rituals to be performed. The feathers are pinned on the mat covering the house for, or against enemies; consecrated water is put into the hands of affected person and other people around to put on their head and rub on their body as a final cleansing exercise. The above exercise starts in the evening and continues throughout the night and is finalized the following day. The ceremony is done by singing and dancing around the sacred house by all members present at the ceremony.

TAI-YA-AH: A KONO WORD FOR SOLAR ENERGY

All symbols depicting the serpentine form is symbolical of motion that represents the solar energy in one of its many forms. The sea dragon, which the Kono call Ngareh (Mammy-water*)*, represents the solar energy in one of its many forms. Thus, it represents the Solar life force imprisoned in water, such as the rivers—**Baffin, Bayah, Bagbeh** in the Kono District and it also represents the divine energy coursing through our human bodies as the *Kundalini or the serpent* *fire at the base of the spine*, which may manifest in some people in its greed, passion and lust. Yes, the Kono worship the bird in various forms, such as under rocks, trees or forests but this is not different from worshiping the same in churches or temples as supported by the ancient Egyptians.

PART V

CHAPTER ONE

The Damby Animals as Identified by the Ancient Kono Primogenitors

NOTES ON THE KONO DAMBY TRADITION A GREAT REALITY

We see the religious belief system of the of ancient through the filters of the secret societies, in particular; the Poro, Sandaih, the Sumoeh, other cults (cultures) and the theology of immortality or life after death. Consequently, much of the marginally related, but nonetheless significant, material has been lost, stolen and duplicated or overlooked. The Great Cults of the Ancestors, the mythological framework in which the Damby Philosophy-Theology functions and gains expression, was unstated; perhaps because it was secret, jealously held by the Elder Initiates, or possibly because it was so well known as to be universal. Recovery of this lost Great Knowledge supplies a pattern in which the chaotic pieces of the Kono Philosophy can be comfortably accommodated. For this and other reasons, I undertook this tedious task with the hope that other Kono may join me on this venture

To conceal the truth about Jesus and still illustrate the point from the ignorant, the Mystery School used many strange creatures. For example, Kenealy, in his Book of Enoch, he depicted the *Caterpillar* as a symbol of the Messiah. To the Kenealy, the Caterpillar creature symbolizes a lowly creeping and wholly terrestrial aspect. But others associated the animal with spinal column, the Serpent, Salmon Scarab, Peacock and the dying Dolphin.

BEE: the symbol of industry.

INSECT The habits of insects were also carefully studies:

This was a symbol of the spinal fire which according to the Egyptian Mystery Schools, it destroyed when it was permitted to gather at the base of the spine and thus, representing the tail of the Scorpion.

ANT *(TUM-BU-U)*; A Kono word for the **ant** for insect. **and** symbolizes industry and foresight as it stores up supplies for a rainy day, or winter, also, its strength of moving objects many times it size or weight.

LOCUSTS (*KON-DO-NE-NU*); a Kono word for: the **LOCUSTS.** The characteristic style of the locusts sweeping down in clouds on Africa rice farms, obscuring the sun and destroying everything green were considered *fitting emblems of passion, disease, hate and strife.* For the emotions destroy all that is good in the soul to the point of causing emotional bankruptcy.

SCARAB, the King of the Insect Kingdom. Symbol of bodily strength, the resurrection of the soul and the Eternal and Incomprehensible Creation in His aspect as Lord of the Sun. The Egyptian Scarab is one of the most remarkable symbolic animal ever conceived by the human mind. The ancient priests' choice of this animal must have been based on specific reasons rather than its simple peculiar habit and appearance, the strength of the body, the resurrection of the soul and the Eternal and Incomprehensible.

THE CREATOR IN HIS ASPECT AS THE LORD OF THE SUN: WHY THE EGYPTIANS WORSHIP THE SCARAB

"Yet another view held in ancient times was that there was a vast meadow over which a huge beetle was carved, pushing the disk of the Sun before him. This beetle was the sky-god and arguing from the example of the beetle, which was observed to roll along with its hind legs a ball that was believed to contain its eggs.

The early Egyptians thought that the ball of the Sky-God contained his egg and that the sun was his offspring. But there were others that state that the ball which the beetle rolls along contains not its eggs, but its dung that is to serve as food for its eggs, which it lays in a carefully prepared place.

The Scarab was the emissary of the sun, symbolizing light, truth and regeneration. Stone scarab, called meant Scarab, about three inches long was placed in the heart cavity of the dead when that organ was removed to be embalmed separately as part of the proves of mummifying.

RA, THE GOD OF THE SUN HAD THREE IMPORTANT ASPECTS:

1. As the Creator of the universe he was symbolized as the head of a Scarab and was called Khepera, (*Kai-fa-ah, Kai-pharah, Kai-phaia*) which signifies resurrection of the soul and a new life at the end of the mortal span.

2. The Scarab has beautiful concealed wings under its glossy shell typified as the winged-soul of man hidden within its earthly sheath. The Scarab was used also as a symbol of civility, strength and courage because the Egyptians believe they were all of the male sex. Hence the name *Kai-pha-ah, Kai-phaia, or* Khepera, meaning second male

3. According to Plutarch—the Scarab rolled its peculiar ball of dung backwards. While the insect itself faced the opposite direction. Thus, it was made a fitting symbol for the Sun, because this Orb (according to Egyptians, astronomy was rolling from the West to the East, although moving in the opposite direction).

An Egyptian allegory states sunrise is the result of the Scarab unfolding its wings, which stretch out as glorious colors on each side of its body. The solar globe that it folds its wings under its dark shell at sunset, night follows.

Khepera, the Scarab-headed aspect of Rah is sometimes symbolized riding through the sky. This is the God of the Sky riding in a wonderful ship called the Boat of the Sun.

SCORPION, *SPINDAI-EH*; A Kono word for symbol of both wisdom and destruction. The Egyptians called it the accursed creature. The emblem of Judas Iscariot—the betrayer. Since the Scorpion stings with its tail, it was called a backbiter, a false and deceitful thing. The scorpion is emblematic of the wicked and the symbol of persecution. **SCORPION**—the great betrayer.

NIGHT MOTHS; Typifies sacred wisdom, because they are hard to discover and concealed by the darkness (ignorance). Some are emblems of death called the *death's head moth* which has a marking on its body that looks like a human skull.

DEATH WATCH BEETLE; The Death Watch beetle was said to give warming of pending death by a specific ticking sound is an example of insects' involvement in human affairs.

SPIDERS (*TEH-TEH-EH*); Due to its shape, the Mysteries schools use the spider to represent the nerve plexus and ganglion of the human body.

PLANTS, ANIMALS AND MINERALS; Certain plants, minerals and animals have been sacred among all cultures of the world because of their specific sensitivities to the astral fire—a mysterious agency in Nature which the scientific world has contacted through its manifestations as electricity and magnetism.

Magicians and witch doctors in Africa and other cultures for instance, surround themselves with animals such as snakes, monkeys, leopards, etc., because they were able to appropriate the life forces of these species and use them to the attainment of their own ends.

A good example here is the legend of Spider Man or Woman. Among the American Indians, the spider's web connected the heaven and the earth.

There are African legends that depicted certain gods who worked with the universe during its creation in connecting the realm of light with those of darkness by means of webs. Hence in our time, we now communicate globally through the web systems called TV, Internet or wireless systems.

Thus, the builders of the Cosmic System who held the embryonic universe together with threads of invisible forces were sometimes called Spider Gods.

HONEY BEE (*KHUMI-NEH*); a Kono word for Honey. The Bee is a symbol of wisdom because of the fact that the bee collects pollen from flowers, so mankind extracts wisdom from experiences of daily life.

The bee was sacred to the Goddess Venus, thus, it was one of the many forms of lies which came to the earth from the planet Venus several million years ago.

WHEAT, RICE AND BANANA; These food sources were said to be of the same origin as the bee. And this is the reason why their origin cannot be traced. The fact that the bees are ruled by queens is one of the reasons why this insect is considered a sacred feminine symbol.

The Hindu God, Prana—the symbol of the universal life force is sometimes shown surrounded by a circle of bees. Since the bee is significant in palletizing flowers, it is the acceptable symbol of the generative power.

In medieval times, the bee was the emblem of the French Kings. The Kings or rulers of France wore robes embroidered with bees and the canopies of their thrones were decorated with gigantic figure of bees.

FLY (*SI-I-SA-AH*): a Kono word for the *Si-i-sa-ah*, also interprets to mean *to sing a song*, may be due to noisy buzzing or humming sounds of the fly.

The fly symbolizes *tormentor* because of the annoyance it brings to animals. The Chaldean god, Baal, was often called Basal-Zebul, or the God of the dwelling place. The word, Zebub or Zabab, means a fly.

In the Kono language, the word Sie-sa means *fly*, but the word can also mean to *sing a song*—the *Song of Sa*, the death god. Baal-Zebul, on the other hand, means Baalzebub or Beelzebub, a word which came down to us to mean Jupiter's fly, note here that the Kono word for Jupiter is Sah.

The ability of flies to destroy decaying substances to promote health depicts the fly with a form of divine power.

The fly got its name, Zebub (Si-a-boh) a Kono word to *sing a song* from its unique buzzing or humming sound . . . Some believe that the Jewish word, Baalzebub, meaning my Lord of the Flies means *My Lord who Hums or Murmurs*.

According to Inman, in his work—Ancient Pagan and Modern Christian symbolism—New York, 1874—recalls the singing Memnon on the Egyptian desert, a tremendous figure with an Aeolian harp on the top of its head.

When a strong wind blows, this great statue sighs or hums. The Jews changed Baalzebub into Beelzebub, thus, making him their Prince of the devils by interpreting daemon as "demon," in the same way he was able to turn Saa-tan (the Saa you met), to the Satan, the evil one.

REPTILES The serpent was the animal of choice from among the reptilian family as a symbol of the head. *Khun-neh* is a Kono word for a type of serpent or snake, *Khun-neh* is also a Kono word for the head. Almost all cultures both ancient and modern have worshipped the Serpent in one form or another.

Minaneh is a Kono word for Cobra, the cobra is also honored among other cultures such as the Nagas of India, Burma, Siam and Cambodia; and the Biblical narrative of the Brazen Serpent of Moses and the Chosen children of Israel; the mystic Serpent, such as Orpheus, the Snake at the Oracle of Delphi, the Uraeus coiled upon the forehead of the Pharaohs and priests in ancient Egypt; all these support the claim of wisdom.

1. From ancient times, the Serpent entwining a staff was the symbol of the medical profession.

2. The Serpent wound staff of Hermes is the emblem of medical profession.

3. Almost all cultures have accepted the Serpent as the symbol of wisdom and salvation.

Thus, the Christian antipathy towards its snakes is due to ignorance of the true meaning of the word serpent, especially the allegory of the Garden of Eden.

The Serpent of the Biblical narratives corrects and tempts mankind to the knowledge of him or herself. This knowledge of ourselves became mankind's obedience to the Demiurge God Jehovah.

HOW DID THE SERPENT COME TO BE IN THE GARDEN OF THE LORD ANY WAY?—

If all God has declared to be good was good—including all creatures, which He had made during the six days of creation to be as good as God then why is the serpent evil?

This portion of the Genesis needs to be examined by all those who are zealous to take God's words to the four corners of the world.

IS THE TREE THAT GROWS IN THE MIST OF THE GARDEN THE SPINAL FIRE?

Image # here

The knowledge of the use of the spinal fire was the spinal gift of the Great Serpent. Note here that the Serpent is the symbol and prototype of the universal Savior Who redeems the world by giving the Creation the knowledge of self and the realization of good and evil.

Not with standing the validity of this claim, then why did Moses and Jesus raise the brazen serpent upon the cross in the wilderness that all who looked upon it might be saved from the sting of the lesser snakes?.

Was the brazen Serpent or prophecy of the crucified Man or Woman to come?

If the serpent was a thing of evil, then why did Christ of no evil introduce his disciples to be as wise as serpents?

The Evil side of the Serpent cannot be substantiated for the serpent as being represented as the emblem of immortality. It is the symbol of reincarnation, metempsychosis because it sheds its skin annually, reappearing in a new body.

The violence and genocide in Africa is based on a Westernized ancient superstition that snakes never die except by violence and injury and that they can generate their lives and live forever.

Black people are regarded by non-black cultures, ancient or modern as *children of the Serpent: thus, they never die. This is the reason why Africa is the prime stage for violence.*

One thing, you the reader must remember here is that the rich or the elite tend to use the religious sector to satisfy their own images.

According to H.P. Blavatsky (Isis Unveiled) "Before our globe had become egg-shaped or round, it was a long-tail of cosmic dust or fire mist, moving and writhing like a Serpent: the Spirit of God moving on Chaos, until its breath has incubated Cosmic matter and made it assume the annular shape of serpent with its tail in its mouth, emblematic of eternity in its spiritual and our world in its physical sense.

SERPENT,*THE SEVEN-HEADED SERPENT*;

This serpent represents the Supreme Deity manifesting through His Seven Spirits, by whose assistance He establishes His Universe. The coil of the Serpent symbolizes motion such as the orbits of the celestial bodies and is probable that the symbol of the Serpent twisting around the egg represents the apparent motion of the Sun around the earth and the bands of astral light. Here, again we find the Kono staying with the game of knowledge. In their naming tradition, there are seven names for males and seven name for females, the name Mani starts the seven naming system. The key word here is *Man*. Did Bible tell us that god said *"let us make man . . ."?* We are also told that *seven* like the name *Mani* is a number of completion.

ELECTRICITY, *AS A SYMBOL OF THE SERPENT*; Because of its motion, electricity was used in the ancient by the ancients as an emblem of the serpent because electricity passing between the poles of a spark gap seems serpentine in its motion.

Force projected through atmosphere was regarded and called the Great Serpent. The Serpent is the symbol of the Universal force, thus, the serpent was the emblem of both good and evil—hence, a force can destroy as quickly as it can build.

The symbol for eternity is symbolized by a serpent with is tail in its mouth—for in this form, the reptile has neither beginning nor ending—*"My beginning is my end and my end is my beginning.*

The head and tail of the serpent represents positive and negative poles of the cosmic life circuit. The initiates of the mystery schools called themselves serpents and their wisdom was considered parallel to the divinely inspired power of the snake.

THE WINGED SERPENTS: the seraphim were the title given to the unseen hierarchies that worked with the Creator in Creation of the Earth. *The symbolic relationship between the Sun and the Serpent is due to the fact that the Serpent does not die until sunset and this fact does not change even if the Serpent was cut up in many pieces.*

LIZARDS, *DAI-YA-AH*: a Kono word for

Lizards are symbols of Mercury due to their rapid motion. Mercury was known as the Messenger of the Gods, whose winged feet traveled infinite distances instantaneously.

CROCODILES *(FA-YE-EH)*; a Kono word for:

The Egyptians and most African traditions regarded the Crocodiles as symbols of Typhon (Water Spirit), and emblems of the Supreme Deity of the latter because while under water, the crocodile sees through thin membrane covering its eyes. It is believed that the crocodile can foretell the future.

There are two types of crocodiles—the largest and more ferocious which was hated by some e.g., Egyptians, which they parallel with Typhon, the demon that destroys.

The crocodile is what the Kono call *Fa-yee* (father water). The good, tamer, and smaller crocodile was liked by the ancients. This is the one the Kono call Bamba / alligator. It is the personification of Good. Thus, it gives the Kono two Damby groups: the Bamba groups all males of the crocodile clan, and the Pengusa: all females of the crocodile clan.

However, it is not clear why the females of this clan should be assigned the pig as their totemic animal. Thus, it is this author's suggestion that the pengusa group posit a scientific question that calls for further studies . . .

THE TURTLE (*CHO-OH*); a Kono word for

The Chinese as well as other African tribes regard the turtle as the symbol of longevity. The turtle is a symbol of wisdom because it retreats into itself and is its own protection. It is also a phallic symbol, as its relationship to long life would prove. The Hindus depicts the universe as being supported on the backs of four great Elephant who, in turn, are standing on an immense turtle which is crawling continually through Chaos.

SIA: THE ANCIENT EGYPTIAN MEANING OF THE WORD;

Sia as a god personifies the perceptive mind. He was created from blood dripping from the phallus of Re, the sun god. In the Old Kingdom, Sia is visualized at the right side of Re and responsible for carrying the sacred papyrus whose contents embody intellectual achievement. On the walls and ceilings of tombs in the Valley of the Kings, Sia travels in the boat of the sun god. He was the spokesman of the sun god in the Books of the Sky (Heavens) (thus the Kono called her Sia Banda: Band-ah is a Kono word for heaven) and the herald who stands at the bow of the solar bark in the Book of Gates.

Sia, who was part of a complementary pair consisting of Sia and Hu, is probably equated with the intellectual energies of the heart of Ptah in the Memphite theology, resulting in the creative command of Path's tongue. However, it appears that Sia never benefited from a cult in his honor. For the Kono however, Sia maintained her ancient status hence, Sia is the name of the first female according to the order of the mother's pregnancy.

PART VI

INTRODUCTION

The Names and Characters of the
Kono Damby Animals

EGYPTIAN IDEAS: TOOLS AND SYMBOLS OF RESURRECTION

These were the tools and symbols that helped in shaping the Kono belief system.

The Egyptians had devised a myth, which was enacted in the heavens yet paralleled in common human experience. They used certain symbols to communicate to other initiates regarding the three Aspects of consciousness use by earthly humans on planet Earth.

These Ancient Egyptian Symbols are globally used to depict: **1**, an animal that resides under ground, **2**, one animal that walks on the earth, and **3,** one animal that flies over the earth; and they then formulated symbols to represent each of these three animals. In terms of human consciousness, these animals reflected certain aspects of the Brain.

These ancient experiences enacted by the Kamu/Egyptians left significant marks on the African cultures as a whole. Many of the Slaved Africans that were stolen from out of Africa and carried across the Atlantic did not leave their cultures behind; and were able to preserve this even under the odds of humanizations.

"You stand in your tomb in the morning
To see the Aten when he rises, you wash
Yourself and clothe yourself as you did

When you were on earth . . . You arise . . .
Freshly animated"

Therefore, African Traditional religions are the motivating and energetic force of all African peoples that was first to find expression in their land of bondage.

The slave master was able to claim the body of the slave *but never* the Africa World view of the African, which was *nurtured and etched* in his or her very soul. Visit Jamaica, Brazil Haiti and so on and you will find traces of African religion running through the veins, the thread that links us all called by the Western minds the Bloodline.

CHAPTER ONE

Leopard Totemic Groups

LEOPARD TOTEMIC DAMBY

Sawa, Koawa, Tongoe

There are three main groups among the Leopard totemic groups known as **Kwie-ta-na-tinu** as follows:

1) *Sandu-U-Nu,* groups in Gbenseh Chiefdom
2) *Koawao,* in Sandur Chiefdom
3) *Tangoeh-Nu,* groups in Tankoro or Tango-oh Chiefdom
4) *Sawa-Nu, groups in Soa*

KWUI-YEE-TANATINU:

KUWI, the Kono word for LEOPARD

A leopard is a large spotted cat with a large slender body and a member of the cat family with a yellowish brown to orange red coat spotted with black rosettes skin. The Leopard is also known as **the Panther and** Symbolic of power and strength. Many tribes in Africa wear the ritual skin to bring strength to the wearer.

LEOPARDS AND LIONS IN HUMAN FORM
WHO WALK LIKE MEN

Animals are used in all cultures of the world because all human beings share some form of characteristics with them. Therefore, it is no surprise to find Animal Secret Societies in all cultures. All animal societies, such as the leopard, the lion societies, crocodile, serpents and other animal societies are cloaked in mystery and secrecy, to protect their secrets from the profane and non-members. These societies are the guardians of the culture and the society itself. They have played a great role in history and their power is far reaching. They predated the colonial period and were the bulwark: that fortifies or protects their communities by building their mystical powers like walls around their communities.

These societies viewing themselves as the rampart or as the tree trunk that unites the roots, the branches, as well as leaves, shouldered the responsibility, economical, social and other welfare of their communities.

Therefore, in Africa, during the European invasion of Africa, these secret societies viewing themselves in such a light empowered them to assume a greater role which allowed them to prevent European colonialism from making inroads into the main lands.

One such society was the Poro of the Kono and the Mendes of Sierra Leone, West Africa, who used the power of their secret societies to win the war against the British through the use of coded languages that were foreign to the Europeans.

Through the same means, they also prevented the British advancement into the provinces during the colonial era, via the use of coded languages, such as, for the Kono, the code word was Waima, which interprets to mean *the general meeting was going to be held at the township of Waima*. For the Mendes, the codes was *n'goyah,* which means one for all or all for one or simply, 'One Word.

The key issue is not how the natives used animals to personify themselves to avenge themselves against their enemies. The intriguing question is how they used the scientific knowledge to transform themselves into animals to achieve their objective in defending themselves against invasion.

The answer to these question baffled scientists because of their intense research methods, but the natives did not use those methods—they achieved what they wanted through nature itself.

The scientists view these transformations as marvels—how did these people act and behave like animals? If a leopard man wears the cloak of a leopard—he behaves and acts like one. The same principle applies to the serpent man.

The leopard is highly regarded by many cultures and tribes. In ancient and modern times, Leopards are considered as emblems or symbols of divinity. In ancient Egypt, if a leopard crosses your path, that person has leadership qualities. Most Africans, believe that there are animal guides for their final resting place.

Leopards have strong bodies and necks. They hunt at dusk and dawn, stalk steadily and have a keen sense of sight—six times as strong as humans and hearing twice that of a human.

The impressive Leopard Totem possesses the following virtues:

Independence, sense of freedom, psychic-sight, fearlessness, integrity and dignity.

THE CLOAK OF THE ANIMAL

The cloak of the animal symbolizes men who personify their own inner animals. These men of power actually became the animal. They can or may live in the body of a leopard, lion or baboon.

To reach these higher levels of transformation, they have to abide by a strict code of secrecy. Not even under penalty of death, must they reveal the secrets of their brotherhood, which involved secret signs and passwords, ritual symbology and special languages through which, members communicates with one another, for example, two leopard members can easily convey messages and still have another meaning to the ears of those who were not a part of the secret society.

This language that was inside the greater society, involved animal calls and a host of other physical standards, which served to bind the group.

Sacred clothing was sometimes used, along with traditional weapons, such as claws and special knives.

They used weapons akin to the animals they tried to identify with. These items would be used to eliminate certain people who were opposed to the secret society as a whole.

The human leopard would be so transformed by assuming the persona of a leopard that one would think it was done through the use of supernatural forces and it would be hard to distinguish a transformed human Leopard's work from that of an actual leopard. When someone of the leopard society was sent on a mission, they would leave tracks and wounds appearing to be the result of leopard claws and teeth. However, it must be remembered that these animal societies are not the same as the Damby, clan or totemic tribes, which is the core of this book. In other words, these animal societies can act like any other gang society, *such as the Mafia, or the Mexican Familial Groups.*

However, these societies find their origin in the Damby, clan or similar type society during the time humans had tried to identify themselves into groups based on the founding fathers of the Damby clan or totemic group.

Those animal societies described above were reverenced as warriors. Thus, this homage to the ancient warrior gods by the priesthood eventually gave birth to the leopard and lion societies of East and West Africa.

The Africans believe that the knowledge of the animal societies came from the deities themselves through the spiritual systems. Warriors of extraordinary martial skill empowered by the deity would perform miraculous feats of strength and endurance admits other manifestations of supernatural power.

Dramas of an initiatory nature were performed only in the proper season to harmonize with the universal forces. The main emphasis is not on developing techniques, but the principles upon which those techniques are founded. Also developed was a fighting consciousness within the nature of man through divine principles.

Warriors were initiated through various rituals, usually at a very young age, through which they were blessed and sanctified to the clan animal.

This warrior was taught the sacred dances, music and songs to revoke the state of consciousness of the Great Elder: the first lion or leopard or other Totemic animals from which the group identifies with.

ANIMAL SYSTEMS AND SHAPESHIFTING

The body's organs are the divine receptors for the animal souls. The Energy activated by the will, enabled the warrior to transform or shape-shift into the clan animal.

According to *James Chuchward, author of the Continent of Mu* states that the totem of Prince Coh, the brother husband of Queen Moo (Mu) depicts the Seven Serpent heads, the symbol of the Can dynasty. Thus, Queen Mu and Prince Coh are of the CAN dynasty. Can is the same as Kah, meaning snake or serpent.

For instant, the belief in animal totems such as the Leopard had empowered men to perform the impossible things which they would not normally perform until the animal transformation or form is invoked . . .

CHAPTER TWO

Pumpkin: Totemic Family Known as Gbei-Yee Tanatinu or Komane-Nu and the Kono Word for Pumkin is Gbi-ie

KOMA NEH: TOTEMIC FOODS ARE= VIPER, PUMPKIN, DUIKER

The various shapes of the pumpkins speak for themselves and indicate why the Ancients chose the pumpkin as a totemic food. These various shapes drives us back to the Sacred Geometry, such as the Circle, the Dot, the Square, the Line, the Seed as an emblem of Eternity so presented, pregnancy is also depicted in the roundness of he pumpkin. The reader can make his own spiritual interpretation and this is reason for his spiritual growth.

CHAPTER THREE

The Otter Totem

Foadu, Yokone   **Otter, all rodents, honey**

The Kono word for the animal called the Otter is *Kunguneh*, the sound mage the otter as it accompanies by riding on the back of the crocodile. In this respect, the Otter or Knuguneh acts as a sort of Serine to announce the presence of the King of the Water call by the Kono *Fayee*, meaning Father or King of the Waters, and also a Kono name for the Crocodile as already explained above and else where in this book. Since this animal is always in the company of the Crocodile, it has become a fitting prohibition to the Fayeetanatinu or *Bambanu*.

CHAPTER FOUR

The Origin of the Kono—Egyptian Connection

BUFFALO TOTEM: *SIE-YOR-EH-NU OR SI-IE-TANA-TI-NU*

COW—Nin-gee
(Nin-gee is the Kono word for cow:
**[*Nin is a variant form of nun, which means hidden;*

Gee means water or mind. Putting it together, Nin-gee actually interprets to mean the hidden waters or mind of the Great Mother, the Giver and Preserver of Life through her milk giving Power]

Who knows or who has found the hidden secrets in the Mother's Milk or the Great Mother's Mind—in other words, the secret life-giving force of the Universe?

The ancient understood that this 'milk' has saved them by causing Hathor to become drunk on blood.

Perhaps, the most common manifestation of the Great Mother as Preserver was the white, horned milk-giving Moon-cow, still sacred in India, and other cultures as a symbol of Motherhood.

Egypt revered Mother Hathor as the heavenly cow, whose udder [*mammary of cow, sheep, or goat:] a bag-shaped structure containing two or more milk-secreting glands, each with its own teat, found in mammals such as cows, sheep, and goats]* produced the Milky Way, whose body was the firmament; and who daily gave birth to the sun, Horus-Ra, her Golden Calf. The same deity worshiped by Aaron and the Israelites. *"These are thy gods, O Israel, which brought thee up out of the land of Egypt"* (Exodus 32:4-14.). Perhaps one of the main cult objects associated with HARTHOR: goddess of dance, the kono word **Adonn-n** meaning to dance is derived from the same name of *Yah-tor, Yah-a-dohnn,* and Kono word meaning to-dance with the Lord, lion or to play with the eye.

All Europe was named after the Goddess as a white Moon-cow, whom the Greeks mated to the white bull incarnation of Zeus. Her alternative name was Io, Kao, or kau, the Moon.

Under the name of moon, she was presented in classic mythology as a rival of Hera, a Greek goddess. However, patriarchal writers always set different manifestations of the same Goddess at odds with one another; possibly on the principle of divide and conquer, principles depicted i. e . . , 'the cow jumps over the moon' nursery rhymes which was really pointing to the direction of the movement of religion from the control of females represented by the ancient Egyptians to that of all males' religions represented by Judaism, Christianity and other male oriented religions like Islam. The cow represents the male while the moon represents the female. Conversely, the cow-moon scenario also meant that the religion of Abraham or Aaron depicted as the moon was been compared to the Egyptian religion depicted as the cow and represented by Sarapis.

Hera herself was named Io, ancestress of the Ionians. In her temple at the site of Byzantium, she appeared as the same lunar cow, the Horned One, wearing the same crescent headdress as the Egyptian Cow goddess.

The ancient Konos called her, *Tegbeh*, due to her crescent headdress. Her other name was *Bundy-N'-yah or simply Bundy, which means loaded or basket goddess of goodness carried on one head or a symbolical representation of the world being carried on the Great Mother's head.*

In the Kono tradition, the word *Bundy-N'yah or Bundy* is usually added to the name of the first female child, according to the Mother's pregnancy, for example: Sia Bundy, because she's a symbolical duplicate of the Great Mother. Bundy is a symbolical obligations conferred on the first female of the Mother as a direct transfer of spiritual duties or spiritual responsibilities of the Mother Creator.

This Kono concept of the basket on the head or Bundy parallels the Pandora Greek mystery, which, in fact, is the direct interpretation of what happened in history, when the Greeks stole the legacy of the African/black mystery teachers. They made those stolen legacies theirs, without fully understanding their truth values. Thus, by opening the truth to the world through ignorant teachers or misinformed teachers is likened to opening the *Pandora Box of Evil*. And all history attests to this fact.

It's ironic that during election time, the truth about the Pandora Box is revealed, when candidates start revealing the truth about each other. In the Kono culture, there is a saying that *if you don't know how" you were given birth to," you should run for an election.*

The Cow, as a creature was equally prominent in myths of northern Europe, where she was named Audumla; she was also Freya, or a Valkyrie taking the form of a fierce cow. A semi-patriarchal Norse myth tried to attribute the creation of the world to the giant Ymir, whose body and blood made the universe, but he was not the first of creatures. The Cow preceded him, for he lived on her milk. Yee-ma or Ymir is a Kono word for the Mind of the Great mother or the breath of her Consciousness . . .

Earlier myths showed the universe being "curdled" into shape from the Cow's milk. In India, many still believe literally the creation myth known as Churning of the Sea of Milk. The Japanese version said the primordial deep went "curdle" (koworokowor) when stirred by the first deities, to make clumps of land. The ancient Near East thought human bodies too were curdled from the Goddess's milk. One of her liturgies was copied into the Bible. "Has thou not poured me out as milk, and curdled me like cheese? (Job 10:10).

The root word for "cow" was Sanskrit *Gau*, Kono and Egyptian *kau* or *kau-t*. Goddess-names like Gauri and Kauri also designated the yonic cowry shell, which is a very important element in the twin rituals among the Kono Tradition.

Braham rebirth ceremonies used either a huge golden yoni or an image of the Cow-mother. "When a man has for some cause been expelled from his caste, he may be restored to it after passing several times through the belly of a cow.

The Egyptian Goddess as birth-giver typically wore a cow's head or horns, as she offered breasts with both hands. As the nursing mother, who gave each Egyptian his secret soul-name (ren), she was entitled Rennet, the Lady of the Double Granary, and a reference to her inexhaustible breasts. God).

A favorite Roman emblem of the Goddess was the *Cornucopia*, Horn of Plenty, a cow's horn pouring forth all the fruits of the earth. The cow was honored as the wet nurse of humanity. As will be seen later, the horn of a buffalo or a cow is a *tana or totemic* object in the Kono tradition. *See the list of totemic animals below.*

The head of a cow looks like a fallopian tube, a female reproductive organ, (frontal view of the tube). The example of such a cow is the white horned, milk giving Moon-Cow, which is still sacred in India as a Symbol of Kali—the Hindu Goddess. Egypt paid homage to mother Hathor as the heavenly cow which provides them with milk. *Ninsia-Nin-Sia*, was the ancient Kono name which became *Nin-gi-nan-nga,* a Kono name for the Rainbow with its Seven colors which is represented by the first seven paired names of Kono children in their naming tradition. *Exodus 32:4*—"seems to support the claim of the Goddess Hathor. In fact, the word Hathor for the Kono God is Atoeh, *Yata, or Yator* (the name of God).

[The word *Yata* means 'the Fire God you met', while the word 'Yato'r' could be interpret to mean 'the name of the God or the God you left behind in this world after death'—*Yatoh.*]

Most cultures have variant names for the cow, such as *Io. The word Io* in the Kono language means "in the mind or in the waters". *Io*, also sounds like *Hau*—a sacred Poro word for male members of this imitation society. The Egyptian Hathor is always shown with her crescent headdress.

The buffalo is a symbol of abundance and manifestation. Their large heads represent intelligence of a higher order and their solid bodies ground them to the earth. They are the uniting force between the common and the divine and believe that right actions should be joined to prayer.

Both the bulls and the cows have horns as well as humped shoulders. Horns grow out of the head and extend to the sky indicating reach to a higher order. The hump can be a symbol of energy locked within the body.

Buffalos can be unpredictable and dangerous when provoked. Those with this totem need to remember to see the good in all things and not let their frustration store up inside them. The buffalo reminds us to be thankful for our gifts and respect all life forms. It is a symbol of equality, sacrifice and service.

CHAPTER FIVE

Honey Totemic Damby

THE BEE DAMBY IS FULLY COVERED IN VOLUME I OF THIS DAMBY SERIES

HONEY TOTEMIC DAMBY
Known in Kono as YOR-KON-NEH-NU OR KUMINN-TANA-TI-NU

CHAPTER SIX

Kamaahtana-Ti-Nu: The Elephant Damby Totem

The elephant Damby totemic groups Aare *collectively called Kamatanatinu*

Kamaah, is the Kono word for the Elephant, a large animal with long trunk: a very large gray or grayish brown animal with a long flexible trunk, prominent ears, thick legs, and pointed tusks. Native to: Africa, South Asia.

The elephants have always been prized for their power and strength. They possess high strength. Elephants give birth at night and it is a magical moment, which they can share with humans. An elephant when it gives birth, *the baby elephants screams, as if in celebration of life.*

They are able to relax in the company of humans—fifty elephants can sleep around a human camp, provided the human beings can put up with their snoring.

Elephant society is much like human society. When a baby elephant got kidnapped, the female elephants (the strongest and the fattest) got together and invaded the erring elephants and recovered the baby elephant. This shows mother love, forethought, intelligence and objectives. And elephants are also known for their excellent memory. *Elephants never forget* is a slogan. For this reason, they are used in magical art and as talisman, especially for students.

Elephant's tusks point backwards and can be used as weapons. This indicates an ability to uncover secrets.

The Hindu god, Ganesh, the remover of obstacles, is shown with the head of the elephant.

Despite their great weight, they can move noiselessly with a graceful stride. They live for almost 60 years.

HINDU IDEA OF GOD KANESI (TYPE OF ELEPHANT)

Ganesh, also called Ganapati, the elephant headed God of Wisdom and Success is the defender and remover of obstacles and has to be propitiated first before worshiping other Gods. He is one of the sons of Siva and Parvati. He is known as "Sidhi Data" or bestowal of success in the work. His elephant head is believed to be an emblem of wisdom. His head often has one full tusk, while the other is broken. It is said that he lost it in a fight or that he used it to dictate the Maha-Bharata to the sage Vyasa. His mount or standard is a rat, a symbol in Hindu fable of the sagacity and trickery of this world, much like the fox in the west. So it is natural that the rat should first be conquered, then subdued and employed by the being who represents spiritual strength, whom he was bound to recognize as his superior, since his own cunning would tell him that Ganesh would prove a better guide than even his own perspicacity. The three heads of Trimukha Ganesh depict the three states of being inherent in any manifestation, which are named the Guna.

Kanesi, a Kono for the elephant which parallel the Hindu name of Ganesha is known by many bad names by those who do not know Him. Among the Hindus, He is Ganesha, the elephant God of the Hindus. He is the God of agriculture. His name in ancient times was "Lord of the Land and Crops."

CHAPTER SEVEN

The Dog Totemic Family

THREE FAMILY GROUPS: *Manfune, Kawi, Yiminneh-NU*
ANUBIS: THE DOG HEADED GOD OF ANCIENT EGYPT

A dog is a domestic carnivorous animal with a long muzzle, a fur coat, and a long fur-covered tail, whose characteristic call is a bark. And for the Kono, the dog's 'bark' is as good as its name. Therefore, the Kono call the dog; male or female dog, wolf, fox, or other member of the dog family

Wu-u, Woo or A-wu. A wild animal such as a wolf, fox, dingo, or coyote that resembles a domestic dog and belongs to the same family are all call Wu-u or Woo by the Kono. The word Wu-**u, Woo or A-wu** was so significant to the ancient Kono that the name was adopted and later became a Sacred Authoritative Utterance of the Secret so cites deities. Throughout history dogs have been known as protectors and guardians. They hold the energies of unconditional love and teach us its true meaning. For this reasons the ancient decided that the dog Sirius is one of the watchmen of the Heavens, fixed in one place at the bridge of the Milky Way, keeping guard over the abyss into incarnation. The *Dog Star* is a symbol of power, will, and steadfastness of purpose, and exemplifies the One who has succeeded in bridging the lower and higher consciousness

Dogs are intelligent and sensitive. They are able to sniff out dangerous situations accurately and guide us to safety. Psychic gifts have long been associated with dogs, because of their ability to detect subtle frequencies often unknown to mankind. Recently scientists have discovered that dogs possess the ability to detect cancer affected areas of the human body.

The behavior of a dog often reflects the personality of its owner. Through its observation and constant interaction with you, it knows your movements and is a mirror image of who you are.

CHAPTER EIGHT

The Deer Totemic Group

DEER TOTEMIC GROUP
DAIE-NU OR DOMBA-TANATINU:
DEER TOTEM includes DEER SKIN which the Kono call DOMBAH
GBOW-OH AND BUFFALO HORN (SIE-BANAH)

THE KONO WORD FOR DEER IS DOMBAH

According to James Churchward and the legend of Mu, the original home of mankind, man was represented by a deer, called Keh. This author believes that the word Kai, which is the Kono word for man, is derived from the word Kei, which means deer, which is now the present Kono called Dumba.

This author has a famous uncle called Paul Dumba, who was one of the leading pastors in his days and he was married to author's father's sisters, *Na-ko-ma*.

A deer is an animal typically with antlers; this distinguishes these animals by the branched antlers on males. More than forty species of deer exist, of different sizes and with different markings, and they are found wild on all continents except Australia and Antarctica. The Deer teaches us the power of gentleness, acute observation and sensitivity. A deer is in harmony with nature. They are considered sacred carriers of peace and those who have this totem should learn to open their hearts and give unconditional love. Deer possess excellent sensitivity of eyes, hearing. This represents the ability to see what is below the surface and symbolizes strong clairvoyance.

The antler reaches out to higher form of attunement. The number of points of a deer's antlers can be significant for those who have this totem.

Kudu is the Kono word for both *kudu and gnu* and name for a large antelope with a head resembling that of an ox, a short mane, a beard, downward curving horns, and a tufted tail; and native to Africa.

The Gnu is a member of the African antelope family. It lives in herds, often of large size and grazes on the grasses of the open plains. When gnu is disturbed, they will dash away for a short distance and then spin around abruptly to check out what was it that scared them.

In flight, they behave erratically, they prance about and throw up their heels in a wild erratic manner designed to throw the predator into confusion.

The communication through group interaction is one of the skills the gnu teaches us. The gnu is a powerful totem to have. When it appears, get prepared for an awakening of your strengths and weakness. Life is bound to change.

The word *Daienu* refers to a group of people in a Kono family unit who's Tana or totemic prohibition is the Deer, Kudu, Antelope and any other animal in the Deer family. Together these people are also called *Dombah-tana-tinu,* meaning people who are prohibited from eating deer meet or even touch its skin.

Keh (an ancient name for deer) is of deer family, which is depicted by the ancient as the symbol of the first human created see The Children of Mu by Churchward, James. Another deer type symbol also used by the ancient is the Kudu (antelope). From the word, keh, the ancient Konos derived Kai, a kono word for male.

Kudu is a variant name for the antelope also. Thus, when in the Kono society, one may hear Kai-i Dumbah, (meaning the ancient male deer), as in Rev. Paul Dumba.

CHAPTER NINE

Who are Yayanenu Tortoise or Turtle Damby

TORTOISE OR TURTLE DAMBY known as CHO-OH-TANA-TI-NU
is collective called **Yawannuu** *or* **Mongeonnu.**

The goat and the viper or snake Dambies are also connected with Yayannenu depending on geographic location. Therefore I will discuss them in one chapter.

THE WORDS "MONGOE' OR "MONGE-NU

The word "monogenic" contains two Kono words: "Mo" or "Moe", meaning person, and "Gena", means spirit. Thus, the word mon*ogenic [Monugena = spirit of people] which is* controlled by one gene, gena or spirit. This means then that, the word *"monogenic"* describes a characteristic of a person or people that is controlled by one gene or one pair of genes having one sex of offspring and therefore, producing offspring that are all of the same sex. Clearly, I maintain that the word "monogenic" *is derived from the word "Mongoe' or "Mongoe-nu".*

Tortoise, goat

Cho-oh is a Kono word for *tortoise* or turtle, one of the kono Damby Totemic Animals. The family groups whose totemic prohibition is the turtle are collectively called—***Cho-oh-tana-ti-nu or Mongoenu.***

YAYANE-NU
Though originally found in the Sandur Chiefdom where they have a section called "Yayandah" in Kayima the capital of Sandur chiefdom, they are almost everywhere in all African countries starting from Kono District, Tonkolili, Koinadugu, Freetown, the capital city of Sierra Leone.

There are also found in Guinea, Conakry, Kissidugu, Faranah, Banyah, Gbaikaidu and Dabora. In addition, Yayaneh are also found Gambia where they are called Daudah Jawara, the former President of the country as a representative. In Gambia, they are also called, Bangura, Jawara etc. In Mali, the Jawarahs were the first warrior leaders. The city of Mali belongs to the Jawara warriors.

THE TANA OF YAYANENU
The *Yannenu* females are also prohibited from drinking **palm wine**, such as **Manpama** due to fear of childlessness or bareness for females and allergic reaction i.e., rash for the males. Therefore, this group like the Pengusah and Komanenu are gender based. The prohibition from drinking palm-wine or manpama for males stem

from the Primogenitors reasoning: According to legend, during the time of hunger, the scarcity of the staple food such as rice, the group survived by eating what the Kono call **Fu-u**, the heart of the palm Tree. **Fu-u,** been a survival meal, rice substitute, the Primogenitor therefore, thought it wise to preserve it as a prohibition for both males and females, thereby ensuring a steady supply in time of need. **Fu-gbu-u**, palm-wine from the heart of a severed palm tree is another prohibition for this group. The word **Gbu-u** is a Kono word for *endosperm*, which is produced in the *Fu-u*, the heart of the palm tree.

Almost all ancient culture considered the Palm Tree to be the Tree of life, with its androgynous characteristics such as 1) producing, oil especially palm oil, which is emblematic of the menstrual blood shed monthly by females and source children, 2) the milking-color of the palm-wine and thus, representing the breast-milk of the Mother. 3) The *endosperm*, which the ancient man thought, contains his seed or sons. Naturally, he considered the palm tree to be divine. ***One most not eat ones divinity.***

"I am the vine, you are the branches. He that remains in union with me, and I in union with him, this one bears much fruit, because apart from me you can do nothing." (John 15:5).

CHAPTER TEN

The Kono Goat Damby

BATANATINU

BATANATINU IS THE KONO WORD FOR THOSE FAMILY GROUPS WHOSE TOTEMIC ANIMAL IS THE GOAT.

THE KONO GOAT DAMBY: AND THE ANCIENT EGYPT SEX GODS.

In the Kono Damby, Goat Damby is *collectively called Baatanatinu and belongs to two Groups, **Yawanenu and Mongonenu**: Depending on Geographic locations where they live depends on name used. **Their Totemic Animal**s are the Goat and the Tortoise*

The goat and the bull were especially sacred to the Egyptians as representing sexual creative power.

They were not merely symbols of Osiris, but incarnations of him.

Often Osiris was depicted with *large and prominent organs*, as a mark of his supreme power; and models of him in this form, or with a triple phallus, were borne in religious processions by the Egyptians.

The goat and the bull were especially sacred to the Egyptians as representing sexual creative power. They were not merely symbols of Osiris, but incarnations of him. Often Osiris was depicted with large and prominent organs, as a mark of his supreme power; and models of him in this form, or with a triple phallus, were borne in religious processions by the Egyptians.

On certain occasions the women carried such phallic images, and operated them mechanically with strings.

Signs of sex worship appear not only in the many cases in which figures are depicted, on temple reliefs, with erect organs, but in the frequent appearance, in Egyptian symbolism, of the crux ansata.

Cross, the 'ankh' with a handle, as a sign of sexual union and vigorous life.

A Goat is an agile, horned, ruminant animal related to sheep and has backward curving horns, straight hair, and a short tail. The not only supplies humans with food such as wool, meat, milk; it also gave the vocabularies such as lecher: to describe a lustful man, a man who behaves lewdly and lustfully in a way regarded as distasteful. It also gives us the word scapegoat, someone who is **forced** to take the blame for others. There are many different breeds of goats. Swiss goats, Nubian and so on. The mountain goat is note for its surefootedness on high rocky ledges. The goat can link you with past lives associated with Greece because it shows up prominently in Greek mythology.

GOAT OF MEDES
ANCIENT EGYPT SEX GODS

THE GOAT OF MENDES IN ANCIET* ALSO KNOWN AS *BAPHOMET* (the Kono word 'Baah' for may have derived from this name)

The Ancient Mystery Schools both east and west used monstrous figures, which they display outside temples and at sacred groves to scare off anyone who would let appearances alone scare them from higher knowledge. However, Sabbatical Witches look beyond the image and into the symbolism. This is not an "idol" it's a representation of harmony between two polarities.

The Kono call the head of a goat Bakhuneh, meaning Baa's head is here. The word Bacchus, Balaam, Baal or Bakhus in the Holy Bible may be the corrupt form of the Kono word for the goat, "Baah'. Goats hold the energy of abundant nourishment. They show us how to sustain ourselves to remind us that we must develop independence. Because goats attune to nature's energies, they are thus able to maneuver difficult terrain and go where other animals cannot go. This throws emphasis on the uncharged and unexplored areas within us.

His wings represent the element air, the top of his head represents fire, he sits on top of the world, which is the earth, and the element water surrounds him.

Baphomet points to the Full and the Dark Moon. The hand gestures express the perfect harmony between opposite polarities.

The Dark Moon represents our actions and *Our Will to Action* toward our goals. The Full Moon represents the fulfillment of those goals.

Note: It is also a representation of as above so below.

Baphomet's two horns represents duality and the lotus flame that burns between them represents the eternal flame that destroys duality and causes us to see everything as connected to the universe that surrounds us. The flame is symbolic of the light of universal equilibrium. These, the Kono call *"taa-sohr-ah"* and depicted in the costumes: *"du-us-u", the raffia dress* of the personified gods or dieties. The word *"taa-sohr-ah* is what the Hebrew calls "tassel", which are loose threads hanging on the garments of the prayer garments and popularized at the time of Jesus. This was what the 'woman with the' issue of blood' (pregnant woman) touched that effects her healing. The two snakes that face each other at his solar plexus represent the coming together of opposites or opposing forces. This symbol is the Caduceus, which represents eternal life, and the cycle of renewal. The two snakes act as guardians of the Heart Chakra, letting only the pure of heart through. The solar plexus represents our 'Will', the *Chi force* within us. Within the solar plexus there is a circle representing the dome of the heavens, and the star mantle of the earth.

Baphomet is also the lord of the four worlds.

1) Plant: Represented by the Lotus.
2) Animal: Represented by the Goat
3) Sea Creature: Represented by his scales
4) human: Represented by his male and female features (this symbol also represents the union of opposites Yin and Yang)

The Star on his head represents Earth, Air, Fire, Water, and Spirit.

On his right hand, he has the word **Solve** that means, 'to find an answer' or 'explanations'. On his left hand, he has the word **Coagula**, which comes from the word; **coagulate** which means to change from a fluid into a thickened mass, as is the case with the menstrual flow that coagulates to become a baby.

The female breasts symbolize the life—giving essence given to us from The Goddess

The Star of Baphomet comes from the Pythagorean school of Mathematics. Many have missed the association of Pythagoras' name with Python (another form of the Serpent Leviathan). In fact, one of the more Esoteric derivates of Baphomet is "Baphe-Metis," that is, Initiation into Wisdom-Measurement.

The Goat within the symbol is Pan, the symbol of nature itself.

With two points up, the Pentagram symbolizes the natural and healthy venting of emotion. The one point down is the Lightning bolt or ENTROPY which produced the spark of life as we know it.

The most familiar to people is in fact a legal trademark of the Church of Satan but keep in mind that it was not created in this century!

Sabbatical Witches don't use the inverted pentagram with its three points pointing downwards to mean *The Trinity Denied*, nor do we use the two points upwards, to mean *Attack on Heaven*. It stands for the second degree within The Craft.

The Baphomet emblem used by the Church of Satan was neither original to it nor created by ASL. The original Baphomet dates at least as far back as the medieval Knights Templar. The artwork for the current emblem's goat/pentagram first appears in a 1931 book by Oswald Wirth. The complete emblem with the added circles and "LVYThN" Hebrew letters appears on the cover of a book by Maurice Bessy two years before the creation of the Church of Satan. Early photos of The Church of Satan often show C.O.S members using the Bessy book as a photo-prop because of its prominent cover-Baphomet, and he included that book in his Complete Witch bibliography.

The Sigil of Baphomet.

The five symbols (one at each point of the Baphomet) are five Hebrew letters: Lamed (L), Vau (V), YOD (Y), Tau (Th), and Nun (N). These letters spell out the Hebrew word Leviathan (LVYThN)

The Leviathan is associated with the Ouroboros, or Serpent eating its own tail. This use of Baphomet is derived from the Ophites who used the Serpent as a symbol of Wisdom. The Serpent represents the big-bang/crunch of the Cosmos (the simultaneous creation/destruction).

Even more curious is another form of the Sigil of Baphomet.

The only difference is in the letters which, to begin with, do not start from the same position as in Sigil of Baphomet used by Church of Satan. The letters are Beth, Zain, Nun, Resh, and Tsade.

The Black Metal band "The Cradle of Filth" has this symbol on one of their albums, as well as the band "Venom", but no answer as to what the letters are.

Baphomet, The Goat of Mendes, and the forms of it sometimes are referred to as the Horned God, Cernuous, Thanateros, The Great God Pan or Abraxas. It has a fairly long history.

Baphomet represents the sum of all life on the earth. Baphomet, in the form of the horned god is considered by some to be one of the oldest fertility divinities in history. Of course we are talking about its early forms. Some believe that paintings in the cave in Ariege, France represent one of the earliest forms of Baphomet. Obviously, horns are a recognizable feature of Baphomet.

Founder of Baal worship, Nimrod is often represented with a headdress with horns, and Baal worship is where the name "The Goat of Mendes" comes from. Mendes or Mendez is a place in Egypt where the fertility god Baal was worshiped.

How did Baal, represented as bull "evolve" into a goat is not too clear. Apparently any animal with horns "could pass" as the symbol of fertility and power. Kenneth Grant, leader of Ordo Templi Orientis (Order of Eastern Templar) says that the name Baphomet comes from "Bapho Mithras"—son of Mithras. Mithras was old Indo-Iranian divinity mentioned as early as 14 century BC, and in approx. 66 BC its cult reached Roman Empire.

The sigil of Baphomet as we know it today appears first with the Knights Templar.

In the crusades, one group of knights, upon reaching Jerusalem, moved into stables next to the legendary Jerusalem temple, wanting to be next to the temple night and day and protect it.

Hence their name—Knights Templar.

Later on they accumulated great amounts of gold and all sorts of assets which made them richer than some rulers in Europe. Then the rumors appeared that they worshiped the devil. Even today it's hard to tell if some of the stories true, or if it was all just an insinuation to create anti—templar hysteria and take over their wealth.

Some Knights admitted that they worshiped Devil in the shape of Baphomet. Of course, after several hours of torture session, people have a tendency to "admit" more or less everything they are told to, so this can not be considered a reliable proof.

Whatever the case, this is when the "Sigil of Baphomet" first appears.

It should be noted however, that Satanism is not the only religion where some form of Baphomet appears. Wicca had horned god long before the sigil of Baphomet appeared.

Note : Well known Witch Alex Sanders (the so called King of the Witches) used the symbol of Baphomet during his rituals.

The ancient Greek fertility god, Pan was worshiped long before xtianity came to be. It is believed that Pan was used by xtians as a model for the image of Devil as they liked to imagine Him in Middle Ages—horns, tail, cloven hoofs, and goat legs.

Today there are some people within Vaudun and Santeria religions that use some forms of Baphomet. In England and in the USA there are some Witches who are once again using Baphomet as a symbol of the horned God.

CHAPTER ELEVEN

The Baboon Totemic Groups

The Baboon totemic groups are called kama-anu or Kamaah-tana-tinu and their totemic prohibition: chimpanzee, all monkeys or apes.

KOMANENU: The viper Totemic groups are called Komanenu or Ko-oma-neh their totemic animal therefore is the viper which the Kono call Tunfu-u However, there are also prohibited from other foods such as pumpkin, and duiker. This group can also be referred to as Tunfu-u tanatinu or NYENANU, are the iguana and all reptile totemic group are within this totemic prohibition if its strict laws are observed.

Therefore, since the First Lady of Sierra Leone is associated with these groups in name, totemic prohibitions and Chiefdom she represents, she is a prime representative of all three groups, and thus I am discussing them in one chapter.

Koma neh, the food prohibitions are viper, pumpkin, and duiker.

However, they share their totemic prohibitions with other groups i. e., Nyenanu whose tana is the iguana and all reptile totemic groups.

THE FIRST LADY: SIA NYAMAH KOROMA OF SIRRA LEONE IS A FITTING REPRESENTATION OF THE GROUP, HER FATHER, A. A, and KOROMA'S DAMBY

According to the Damby Tradition, the people whose totemic animal is the viper, are called **Komanenu**, and are therefore, automatically prohibited from eating the viper and all other serpents. In extreme cases, this prohibition extends to all reptilian family. Snakes move on their bellies or rib cage (hence we are told that Eve was made from Adam's ribs), *what is the implication here?*

Furthermore, this group is also known as *Ko-o-ma or Koroma*. The totemic prohibition here is besides been the Viper, which the Kono call, *Tunfu*; the group is also, prohibited from 'licking' palm oil from any clay pot. The reason is this: the clay pot is made like a pumpkin, emblematic of the womb or pregnant belly. Thus, this extra prohibition only applies to the females of this group. The violation of these taboo courses according to the ancients is childlessness. The clay pot is emblematic of pumpkin, which represents the womb. Therefore, leaking palm oil (emblem of blood especially, in this case; the menstrual blood is the point) from this pot depicts licking the menstrual blood, which coagulates to become children. Thus, red palm oil in the clay pot symbolizes the menstrual blood in the womb. The clay pot is the symbol *of the womb, thus, it* would be like licking ones own children from ones womb.

KAMAAH-NU

THE BABOON TOTEMIC GROUPS ARE CALLED KAMAANU OR WOH-O-TANA-TI-Nu.
TOTEMIC PROHIBITION: Chimpanzee, all Monkeys or Apes
Collectively, the Kamaah group is called Kaama-nuh.

This Damby group like the Komanenu is also many and scattered all over West Africa. In Guinea and Sierra Leone, they are called Kamara-keh, Kamara (Kamara male) and Kamara-Musu (Kamara-female). In Kono District, they are called Kamaa-nu. Among the Temnes, Susu, Mandingo, Loko, Mende, Yalunkah,

Korankoh, etc., they are called Kamara. In addition, in Mali, Gambia, Guinea-Bissau, Guinea and Senegal they are also called Kamara.

SIA NYAMA KOROMA AND ERNEST BAI KOROMA, PRESIDENT OF SIERRA LEONE WEST AFRICA

"**Sia Nyama Koroma,** born on March 19, 1958-in Koidu Town, Kono District is a Sierra Leonean Biochemist and Psychiatric Nurse. She is the daughter of the first Kono Lawyer and Attoney-general' and wife of Sierra Leone's president Ernest Bai Koroma making her the currently First Lady of Sierra Leone.

She holds a Master of Science in Organic Chemistry from the University of London and a Bachelor of Science in Nursing from the University of London and Fourah Bay College in Freetown. Sia Koroma is a native of Tombodu Village, Kono District in Eastern Sierra Leone and a member of the Kono ethnic group and of the *Kamaah Chiefdom and Damby*.

She is the mother of two daughters, Alice and Danke Koroma.

Sia Nyama Koroma was born on March 19, 1958 into a wealthy prominent political family from Kono District.

Her mother Danke Koroma was a school teacher in Koidu Town and her father, *Abu Aiah Koroma* (*November 28, 1928-March 6, 2005*) was a Lawyer, and was Sierra Leone's Attorney General from 1967 to 1968 under president Siaka Stevens. Aiah Koroma served as the Managing Director of the National Diamond Mining Company based in Kono District from 1976 to 1987. Abu Aiah Koroma was also a Presidential candidate in the 1996 Sierra Leone presidential elections; he won only 4.9% of the vote".

Sia Koroma spent her early years at various primary schools around Sierra Leone as her Father was being posted from one place to another. For Secondary education, she settled at the Annie Walsh Secondary School in Freetown where she graduated as a Science student in 1976.

She proceeded to London for further studies which culminated in her gaining a Masters in Organic Chemistry. She started her working life at the Sierra Leone Petroleum Refinery where she rose to the position of Chief Chemist. Her duties at the Petroleum

Kumba Femusu Solleh

Refinery included routine quality control of petroleum products, management of subordinate staff team and other senior

Thoth as a baboon with the Sun on the head IMAGE #

The word *Ow-oh* is the Kono word for a large ape, with a relatively short but very powerful body and coarse dark hair and native to Africa. The Latin name is Gorilla. *Ow-oh* is also a name for animals such as the Baboon, Ape or Gorilla. The gorilla has an excellent memory and a keen sense of observation. These animals have acute hearing and respond to unusual sounds that are not part of their normal activity. Those with this totem have clairvoyance. They are also great listeners and respond accordingly.

Gorillas have a gentle strength, patience and clarity of vision. Once they create a goal they stick with it until accomplished. Many gorilla people choose professions working with the deaf and dumb. The Ape is a ferocious fighter noted for its mane. It cries at dawn and dusk, the task given by nature to announce the rise and fall (re-birth and death) of the Sun have given it an important role.

BABOON GOD OF ANCIENT EGYPT

THE GOD THOTH REPRESENTED AS A BABOON IN ANCIENT EGYPT.

The name Toth came down to us as the name of ancient Egyptian's god of Wisdom, writing and counseling. He is said to settle disputes between the living, the dead and the gods, and also connected to the souls of the dead. He was depicted most commonly with the body of a man and the head of an ibis bull or c Baboons were very popular in Egypt, and sometimes kept as pets.

Many tomb scenes show the animal led on a leash, or playing with the children of the household. It is believed that some baboons were trained by their owners to pick figs in the trees for them.

The baboon was also much admired in Egypt for its intelligence and also for its sexual lustfulness. Baboon feces was an ingredient in Egyptian aphrodisiac ointments.

Meaning: The baboon held several positions in Egyptian mythology. The name of the baboon god Baba, who was worshipped in Pre-Dynastic times, may be the origin of the animal's name. By the time of the Old Kingdom, the baboon was closely associated with the god of wisdom, science and measurement, Thoth. As Thoth's sacred animal, the baboon was often shown directing scribes in their task. As Thoth was a god of the moon, his baboons were often shown wearing the crescent moon on their head (as shown in the statue above). Baboons carried out Thoth's duties as the god of measurement when they were portrayed at the spout of water clocks, and on the scales which weighed the heart of the deceased in the judgment of the dead.

The baboon had several other funerary roles. Baboons were said to guard the first gate of the underworld in the *Book of That which is in the Underworld*. In Chapter 155 of the *Book of the Dead*, four baboons were described as sitting as the corners of a pool of fire in the Afterlife. One of the Four Sons of Horus, Hapy, had the head of a baboon and protected the lungs of the deceased.

As mentioned earlier, the baboon was associated with the moon due to his connection with Thoth. However, the baboon was more often considered a solar animal by the ancient Egyptians. This may be due to the animal's habit of screeching at daybreak or because of their practice of warming themselves in the early morning sun. The ancient Egyptians believed these were signs that the baboon worshipped the sun. Baboons were often portrayed in art with their arms raised in worship of the sun. They were also shown holding the *Udjat*, a solar symbol or shown riding in the day boat of the sun-god Re.

Born in times of weakness, when Egypt was regularly invaded and generally controlled by the Assyrians, Dynasty 26 ('the Saite Dynasty') was installed at the head of the tiny kingdoms of Sais and Athribis in the Delta by the Assyrian king Ashurbanipal. This turned out to be a bad move for Assyria. Within 12 years, in an astonishing reversal of fortunes, the Saite king Psamtik would reunify Egypt under his crown and liberate his nation from Assyrian domination. Weaving the clear threat of his military power with extremely agile diplomacy and carefully orchestrated ideology, Psamtek brought about the political reorganization that had eluded his predecessors for four hundred years. At last, Egypt was once again led by a centralized authority—an all powerful king, a guardian of order, a living god. It was a true rebirth for Egypt, with a once again thriving economy, a recovered sense of national identity, and a new-found opening to the outside world—most particularly to the Greek World. Under Psamtik's agile leadership, Egypt was simultaneously moving forward and drawing strength from its glorious past—most particularly that of the Old and Middle Kingdoms.

This was particularly manifest in the arts. Craftsmen of the Saite period aspired to equal, and hoped to surpass, their Middle Kingdom predecessors, while adhering closely to the classic canons of aesthetic tradition—a scenario that would play out again 2200 years later when artists of the Italian renaissance sought to rise to the standards set by their Ancient Greek predecessors. Managing their new prosperity with great skill, while keeping the Babylonians at bay, the Saites embarked on an ambitious program of building, restoring, and embellishing. Commerce flourished under dedicated military protection and ambitious public works projects, such as the digging of a canal from the Nile to the Red Sea—2500 years before the Suez Canal.

Although brilliant by its achievements and the remarkable period of peace and stability it carved within the context of an increasingly turbulent Mediterranean world, the Saite Dynasty was somewhat short-lived (139 years). Its increasing reliance on foreign mercenaries caused tensions, and eventually infighting within the military establishment. Militarily weakened, Egypt became easy prey for the Persian juggernaut. In 525, Persia took over Egypt, putting a sudden end to the Saite period. Egypt would never again shine so brightly.

See Budge, E. A. Wallis, Sir, *1969 The Gods of the Egyptians or studies in Egyptian Mythology (unabridged republication of the 1904 edition by the Open Court Publishing Company). Dover Publications, New York, NY. ([I] 403)*

However, when depicted as a baboon, he symbolizes those creatures that rise early with the sun. Therefore held to be connected to the sun god Ra. Baboons were a feature in early Egyptian festivals (5300-3000 BC); they later became important to the Early Dynastic Kings of Horus (3000—Thoth was also depicted as a lunar god or as a messenger god. He came to be associated with Hermes (see:

Hermes and the Infant Dionysus) in the Ptolemaic period (332-30 BC). 2686 BC).

THE KONO VIEWS ON THE LEVELS OF CONSCIOUSNESS AS DEPICTED BY CERTAIN ANIMALS IN THE DAMBY TRADITION SEE MY OTHER BOOK (*THE PROBLEMS OF FAITH*)

www.ingramcontent.com/pod-product-compliance
Lightning Source LLC
Chambersburg PA
CBHW030312290526
45785CB00001B/323